W9-AZW-685

To Craig

Beauty of the Lord

Awakening the Senses

RICHARD CARTWRIGHT AUSTIN

Dick

John Knox Press
ATLANTA

Abbreviations
ILL Inclusive Language Lectionary
JB Jerusalem Bible
KJV King James Version
NEB New English Bible
NJB New Jerusalem Bible
RSV Revised Standard Version

Library of Congress Cataloging-in-Publication Data
(Revised for book 2)

Austin, Richard Cartwright, 1934-
    Environmental theology.

    Includes bibliographies and indexes.
    Contents: bk. 1. Baptized into wilderness —
bk. 2. Beauty of the Lord.
    1. Nature—Religious aspects—Christianity.
2. Muir, John, 1838-1914. 3. Edwards, Jonathan,
1703-1758. I. Title.
BT695.5.A97 1987   231.7   87-45550
ISBN 0-8042-0869-7 (pbk. : v. 1)
ISBN 0-8042-0859-X (pbk. :v. 2)

© copyright John Knox Press 1988
10 9 8 7 6 5 4 3 2 1
Printed in the United States of America
John Knox Press
Atlanta, Georgia 30365

Dedication

To Anne

We rejoiced together under Ribbon Falls
We have walked together
as far as the Okavango.

Let thy work appear unto thy servants, and thy glory unto their children.

And let the beauty of the LORD our God be upon us: and establish thou the work of our hands upon us; yea, the work of our hands establish thou it.

Psalm 90:16–17, KJV

Contents

Appreciation

Fourteen years ago, in the Grand Canyon, I began to walk with new strength and see with new eyes. I have pursued a Christian pilgrimage since then which has brought me to the experiences and insights I share in this environmental theology. When I began to write, overflowing with ideas and seeking a voice, I was helped by friends who responded to draft chapters: Rose Gallagher, Margaret Gregg, Suzanna O'Donnell, Linda Miano, Dorothy Pike, John Rausch, Catherine Rumschlag, and Arthur Smith.

Robert Handy guided my first studies of Jonathan Edwards, twenty-five years ago. After reading a draft of this book he allowed he was "almost persuaded" by my interpretation of the conversion of this intriguing, elusive Christian philosopher. His comments have helped. I thank Roland Delattre, as well, for his book about beauty in Edwards' thought which inspired me to return to the study of Edwards a decade ago.

George Landes reviewed my use of the Bible in this book and the following one. He cannot be blamed for my viewpoint, but his deep knowledge of biblical languages and context have been helpful at many places.

Robert McAfee Brown preached at my ordination, gracing the beginning of my Christian ministry. When I brought him a very complex manuscript for this study, he helped me find the courage to break it into pieces human beings might bite, chew, and digest.

Edward Smith and I have worked together for five years, he as my therapist. He has supported my desire to integrate body, emotions, and experience into my theological reflection.

Peter Landenbergh, Mandi Upkill Brown, and Batswelelwa helped me experience the Okavango.

Lori Hamm and Ginger Pyron have edited with grace so the reader need not stumble. If anything remains unclear, the fault is mine. I thank John Gibbs for receiving these manuscripts and responding with such feeling.

Anne Leibig, my wife, has been my companion in shaping feelings into thoughts, thoughts into words. Much more than that, she has been my delight. Without delight, this book could not have been written.

Chestnut Ridge Farm
Summer 1987

Acknowledgments

Scripture quotations from the Revised Standard Version of the Holy Bible, copyright 1946, 1952 and © 1971, 1973 by the Division of Christian Education, National Council of the Churches of Christ in the U.S.A. are used by permission.

Excerpts from **The New English Bible** are copyright © the Delegates of the Oxford University Press and the Syndics of the Cambridge University Press, 1961, 1970. Reprinted by permission.

Excerpts from *The Liberation of Life: From the Cell to the Community* by L.C. Birch and J.B. Cobb, Jr., copyright © 1981 Cambridge University Press; *Nature's Economy: A History of Ecological Ideas* by Donald Worster, copyright © 1985 Cambridge University Press. Reprinted by permission.

Selections from *The Function of the Orgasm* by Wilhelm Reich, translated by Vincent R. Garfagno. Copyright © 1973 by Mary Boyd Higgins as Trustee of the Wilhelm Reich Infant Trust Fund. Reprinted by permission of Farrar, Straus and Giroux, Inc. Excerpt from *The Murder of Christ* by Wilhelm Reich. Copyright © 1953 by Mary Boyd Higgins as Trustee of the Wilhelm Reich Infant Trust Fund. Reprinted by permission of Farrar, Straus and Giroux, Inc. Excerpt from *Jonathan Edwards,* edited by Clarence H. Faust and Thomas H. Johnson. Copyright 1935, copyright renewed © 1962 by Hill and Wang, a division of Farrar, Straus and Giroux, Inc. Reprinted by permission of Hill and Wang.

Excerpts from Taylor Stoehr, "Introduction," *Nature Heals: The Psychological Essays of Paul Goodman,* copyright 1977, Free Life Editions. Reprinted by permission.

Excerpts from *Man's Responsibility for Nature: Ecological Problems and Western Traditions* (1974) by John Passmore. Reprinted by permission from Gerald Duckworth & Co.

Excerpts from *Dutton's Point* (1982) by Stephen J. Pyne, used by permission of Grand Canyon Natural History Association.

Excerpts from *The Elusive Presence: The Heart of Biblical Theology* by Samuel Terrien, Copyright © 1978 by Samuel Terrien, RELIGIOUS PERSPECTIVES: ITS MEANING AND PURPOSE, Copyright © 1978 by Ruth Nanda Anshen; *Ecology of Man: An Ecosystem Approach* by Robert

Excerpts from *Lectures on Kant's Political Philosophy* by Hannah
Arendt, © 1982 by The University of Chicago; *American Religious
Thought: A History* by William A. Clebsch, © 1973 by The Univer-
sity of Chicago. Reprinted by permission.

Excerpts from *The Nature of True Virtue* by Jonathan Edwards.
First edition as an Ann Arbor Paperback 1960. Foreword © by The
University of Michigan 1960. Reprinted by permission.

Excerpts reprinted from *Thinking Like a Mountain: Aldo Leopold
and the Evolution of an Ecological Attitude Toward Deer, Wolves,
and Forests* by Susan L. Flader by permission of the University of
Missouri Press. Copyright 1974 by the Curators of the University of
Missouri.

Excerpts from *Beauty and Sensibility in the Thought of Jonathan
Edwards: An Essay in Aesthetics and Theological Ethics* by Roland
André Delattre, Copyright © 1968 by Yale University; THE WORKS OF
JONATHAN EDWARDS, Vol. 1, *Freedom of the Will* edited by Paul
Ramsey, © 1957 by Yale University Press; Vol. 2, *Religious Affection,*
edited by John E. Smith, © 1959 by Yale University Press, Inc.; Vol. 4,
The Great Awakening, edited by C. C. Goen, Copyright © 1972 by Yale
University; *Images and Shadows of Divine Things* by Jonathan
Edwards, edited by Perry Miller, Copyright, © 1948 by Yale
University Press. Reprinted by permission.

An earlier version of some portions of this book appeared in
Environmental Ethics 7 (1985): 197–208, under the title, "Beauty: A
Foundation for Environmental Ethics."

Introduction

Many people today love the world with a perspective that is a novelty in human history, because we see nature and the earth's life-support systems as fragile and vulnerable to human abuse. We worry that we may thoughtlessly damage the earth and we fear that political and industrial leaders may risk the earth's destruction in pursuit of power or gain. The earth has a new beauty for us, a new preciousness.

With the explosion of an atomic bomb over Hiroshima on August 6, 1945, a distinct era in world history began. It is characterized by a growing anxiety that humanity might destroy life on earth or deform life beyond recognition. The most feared scenario is nuclear war among the superpowers, but other fears have also appeared. In 1962 Rachel Carson published *Silent Spring* (Boston: Houghton Mifflin), the first warning that chemical agents utilized by modern technological society might alter, damage, or even destroy natural life processes. After Carson brought the effects of the pesticide DDT to the world's attention, many other environmentally destructive agents and processes were identified— and some have since been controlled. Then in 1968 Paul Ehrlich warned the world of *The Population Bomb* (Rivercity, MA: Rivercity Press), the threat to the earth's carrying-capacity from the rapid growth in human numbers. In 1971 Barry Commoner, writing *The Closing Circle* (New York: Bantam Books, Alfred A. Knopf, Inc.), warned that the consumptive patterns of affluent, technological society are outstripping the earth's resources and may destroy the fabric of life. Each of these writers is a professional biologist with an ecological perspective.

Our traditional culture did not prepare us for the resulting change in our estimation of the earth. We had known nature as the context for human life: nourishing, responsive, challenging, sometimes terrifying. However, we had not realized that life forms and the earth itself are so vulnerable to us. We had not expected their beauty to be so precarious.

In Western culture Christianity has been the major interpreter of life's meaning and purpose. Like other social institutions, though, our churches were not prepared for the change in our perception of the earth. This lack of foresight has generated resentment among some who are frustrated by our society's sluggish response to this new reality and look for a scapegoat. In his famous essay, "The Historical Roots of Our Ecologic Crisis," Lynn White, Jr. claimed that the primary culprit of the contemporary crisis was the traditional Christian affirmation of the right of humanity to dominate nature.[1] White's view is accepted widely, often uncritically, in the environmental movement.

In this book I lay no blame for any institution's failure to prepare us for the dramatic shift in perspective we have experienced since 1945. Rather, I want to help Christians open themselves to a new appreciation of nature so they can fully participate in loving, protecting, and responding to the earth. Anyone may experience nature. Distinctive *Christian experience* of nature, however, is nurtured by Christian faith and in turn feeds Christian understanding. Christian experience of nature, I will suggest, may enhance our delight in the redeeming Lord, may contribute to our personal identity, and may clarify our moral purpose. Also, it may help the earth itself.

To provide a foundation for Christian experience of nature, we first need to inspect and relay some of the building blocks of Christian faith. I see this as a task of remodeling, not new building. I trust the Lord I have known. I have no interest in some new religion which differs from Christianity, for within biblical faith I find resources relevant to the modern crisis of the earth. At the same time I believe that we need to alter significantly some of our traditional perspectives so that we may strengthen the integrity of our faith and enhance its moral beauty.

These changes run deeper than ethics, deeper than learning new patterns of behavior to protect the earth. The changes go to the core of our faith and self-understanding. Aldo Leopold, one of the first prophets of a new environmental perspective, wrote in 1948,

> No important change in ethics was ever accomplished without an internal change in our intellectual emphasis, loyalties, affections, and convictions. The proof that conservation has not yet touched these foundations of conduct lies in the fact that philosophy and religion have not yet heard of it. In our attempt to make conservation easy, we have made it trivial.[2]

Our new perception of the earth's fragility—if it is not trivial, but serious—raises fundamental questions about the purpose of the world and the meaning of human life.

In this book I seek to help readers explore the Christian experience of nature. *Beauty of the Lord* is one of a series which, together, comprise a Christian theology aware of environmental relationships. The first book, *Baptized into Wilderness*, suggests possibilities for a Christian environmental consciousness through the insights of America's earliest prophet for wilderness, John Muir. Muir's conviction—and mine—is that nature has value in itself and in the eyes of God. For spiritual health, people need communion with nature, not just dominion over nature. Following the present book will be a third, developing a biblical understanding of God's delight in nature and the human vocation to care for life. In a fourth book, I will suggest implications for personal ethics, social policy, and agriculture. In *Beauty of the Lord*, however, the focus is on experience. I seek to dissolve theological and psychological impediments to expressive relationships between Christians and natural life.

In the following chapters, I present an image of

beauty to help integrate our experience of God with our self-understanding and our experience of nature. Expressive beauty is at the heart of God, and our faith derives from our experience of this beauty. Faith and self-understanding both gain strength as our senses are awakened for relationships, including relationships with the natural world. The Christian event of "awakening" or "conversion," characteristic in the American religious tradition, may lead to a more creative personal identity; yet human identity is not complete without an affectionate relationship with nature and a sense of moral purpose that reaches beyond human culture to other life. Regard for nature may contribute to the moral beauty of our faith.

*   *   *

I entered the Presbyterian ministry in 1959. Since 1975 I have created an experimental ministry in "environmental theology," seeking to relate environmental concerns to Christian faith. On my mountain farm in southwestern Virginia I grow pick-your-own strawberries, raise grass-fattened beef, and make maple syrup. I assist civic groups with environmental organizing and serve as a resource person to church and conservationist organizations.

Both the Christian nurturing of my youth and my formal theological training stressed the twin pillars of love for God and love for humanity, as well as the duty to devote special care to those with the greatest needs. I was fortunate to receive two of the finest graces which may come through the Christian tradition. First, as a young man I had a clear and moving experience of God's call to faith and to the Christian ministry. Second, I obtained theological training which encouraged questioning and critical reflection. I was a decade into my ministry before I realized that my Christian training had ignored both God's relationship to nature and the ethics of human relationships with the natural world.

When I began my ministry with a "larger parish" of five rural churches in the coalfields of western Pennsylvania, my parishioners began my education about nature. The farmers in these churches overwhelmed me with their stewardship. They would not waste even the wild strawberries growing by the roadside; and when their gardens yielded a surplus, bags of produce appeared mysteriously outside my door. Their engagement with the land was hard-working, unsentimental, yet nourishing. Many lived to great old age, tilling the land as long as they lived. These settled people had three-way marriages: the farmer and homemaker to each other, and each to their homestead acreage. These strong relationships lasted until death.

But farming was retreating as the strip mines advanced. From my hilltop home I could see three "draglines"— giant shovels which ripped the farmland from above the buried seam of coal, depositing rows of rubble. For the single harvest of coal which lay beneath, the land was so ravaged it would never again yield a harvest of corn or hay. Times were hard. Land was cheap, and work was scarce. The draglines roared around the clock, seven days a week. The human operators earned minimum wage while they guided the destruction of the land.

After returning to my home church in Washington, D.C. for three years, I was invited deeper into the coalfields. My family and I moved to the valley of the Big Coal River in West Virginia where I led the Presbyterian Church's largest Appalachian mission project. It was the late 1960s, the height of President Lyndon Johnson's "War on Poverty."

Here there were no farms, but there were miners who taught me more about human love for the land. Their work had been underground, extracting coal in a dangerous communion with the earth. Following work, they had restored their spirits outdoors among the steep, wooded hills that surrounded the "coal camp" villages: hunting, fishing, tending tiny garden patches. Now eight of the nine large underground mines in the valley were closed. In their place the strip mines advanced, creeping round the hills high above the coal camps. Bulldozers cast rocks and trees down the steep slopes. Mud slides crept through the garden patches. Each strip mine worker produced five times the coal that a man underground could mine. This efficiency was purchased with the advancing destruction of mountains and valleys alike. Trees, wildlife, and topsoil were swept away. Once-clear streams were transformed into mud-choked, flood-prone culverts. People's homes were threatened with falling rock, sliding mud, and rising water. Fish were gone, game was fleeing, and even gardens were inundated.

When I arrived people had already begun to fight back. A seventy-year-old Ruling Elder in one church apologized to me for his current preoccupation with the "worldly" struggle against strip mining. A miner and a forest ranger, he loved the land deeply and could not resign himself to what he feared was the proper Christian attitude. Working with many others, he succeeded in getting a strip mining reclamation law enacted in the West Virginia legislature, but the law worked poorly.

Five years later I myself was a leader in this struggle. In 1971 several elected officials asked me to organize a legislative campaign to abolish strip mining in West Virginia.[3] The outcry against strip mining had become the dominant issue in the state. When the state legislature refused to pass such a law, Congressman Ken Hechler proposed federal legislation to abolish strip mining and asked me to work with him.[4] Later, as chairman of the National Coalition Against Strip Mining, I helped organize groups across the country to support federal regulatory legislation. The first time Congress passed a control bill, it was vetoed by President Ford. The second time, I was invited by President Carter to the Rose Garden for his signing of the "Surface Mining Control and Reclamation Act of 1977." Though enforcement was later weakened by President Reagan and Interior Secretary James Watt, the law reduced environmental damage from strip mining.

Without premeditation I had been swept into the strip mining struggle, as I had learned from the people I had been called to serve. I emerged with a desire to focus my ministry on the relationships between Christian faith and the environmental crisis.

* * *

To open Christian experience to nature requires more than "theology" in the narrow sense—more than "rational inquiry into religious questions."[5] I hope to make this theology engaging by anchoring ideas in my own experience. By sharing descriptions of landscapes and even some poetry with the reader, to accompany the development of ideas, I hope to evoke aesthetic and emotional experience alongside intellectual reflection.

My thought has been stimulated by one of America's pioneer theologians, Jonathan Edwards (1703–1758). Edwards expressed an understanding of the beauty of the Lord which led me to the integrating theme of this book. Believing that the sense of beauty is central to human knowledge of God, he considered beauty to be the foundation of ethics as well, because the experience of beauty engages persons with their environment. Jonathan Edwards may have been the most influential Christian thinker and preacher in America's history. As a leader of the Great Awakening, the first vast religious revival to sweep the American colonies, he stimulated the evangelical movement that opened religious participation to ordinary people and brought Christianity to the American frontier. This movement remains the most distinctively *American* expression of Christianity. The Awakening was a religious revolution.

But Edwards was also a leading defender of Puritan piety and Calvinist orthodoxy. A conservative branch of his followers used his writings to protect a type of Presbyterianism which, in the judgment of historian Perry Miller, "became for vast numbers of Americans a *rigor mortis* of the mind."[6] It was Edwards who preached "Sinners in the Hands of an Angry God," the most notorious, inflammatory sermon in American history. He was also the first American thinker to master and use the physics of Sir Isaac Newton and the

psychology of John Locke: he was recognized in Europe as a
brilliant interpreter of both. As a final paradox, historian
William Clebsch places Edwards at the head of a distinctive
American religious tradition which ran to Ralph Waldo
Emerson, the Transcendentalists, and on to William James.
Edwards "resisted the moralistic spirituality" which is
America's chief religious heritage, developing instead "a
consciousness of the beauty of living in harmony with divine
things—in a word, being at home in the universe."[7]

Edwards' psychology was too advanced for his own
generation to appreciate, but it expresses a Christian understanding of human experience which resonates with modern
psychological insights. His philosophy of beauty may help
span the gap between our Christian tradition and modern
environmental sensitivity. Edwards did not himself integrate
nature into Christian experience, but his insights led me
toward this goal.

Flowing through this book there will be a stream of
Edwards' thought, and also a stream of reflection about his
personal experience that illumines limitations to his theology.
Edwards' greatest value as a thinker is that he was also an
actor in a human drama: he applied his theories to life and
then reflected upon the consequences. He left a rich record of
mistakes and accomplishments. I will tap this record to
probe human experience of God.

*   *   *

Modern Western society overburdens the earth in part
because we seek security and satisfaction less in our
relationships with the living and more in the things of our
own manufacturing. Developing moral relationships with
nature will imply, among other things, drawing more
cautiously and thoughtfully from the world's "natural
resources." I do not believe that "self-restraint" will be
adequate motive for such change. If we come to protect the
earth, it will be because we have discovered delights in God,
in ourselves, and in natural life which nourish us without

destroying what we love. British philosopher John Passmore concluded his book *Man's Responsibility for Nature* with a similar observation.

> . . . certainly there is little hope unless we can moderate our desire to possess. We shall do so, however, only if we can learn to be more sensuous in our attitude to the world, more ready to enjoy the present moment for itself, as an object of immediate pleasure, instead of frenetically seeking the power and security that possessions offer.

> It is at this point that the moral outlook of the West is not merely inadequate but dangerous—in virtue of the puritanism it inherited . . . [The] puritan attack on sensuousness, its denial that the enjoyment of sensual pleasures for their own sake can ever be right and proper, has also had . . . ecological consequences . . . Only if men can first come to look sensuously at the world will they learn to care for it.[8]

With help from Jonathan Edwards, America's most influential Puritan, I wish to revive a Christian sensuousness toward God and nature which may help us enjoy and protect this earth.

Part I.

Beauty

"One thing have I desired of the Lord, that will I seek after . . . to behold the beauty of the Lord" (Psalm 27:4, KJV). When King David—lusty, political, self-confident—prayed in these words, he was not pretending that hiding with God was all he desired. He was confessing that his glimpses of the Lord were what made sense of his life. Experience of God clarifies who we are in all our relationships.

This book interprets beauty to join Christian theology with ecological awareness, thus providing a foundation for Christian experience of nature. To know beauty is both pleasing and engaging; it both stirs a response and creates a relationship with a cherished other. Although this understanding of beauty derives from the Christian philosophy of Jonathan Edwards, I depart from Edwards by replacing his Platonism with an ecological perspective. Beauty perceived in nature serves not so much to suggest higher truth as to indicate the value of the life and relationships perceived. Ecology enters this philosophy, as a science interpreting the beauty of the earth, helping us understand the important qualities of natural relationships. The beauty in life-giving relationships is heightened when these relationships support diversity and individuality or span distinctions between beings.

Edwards proposed that beauty is God's most distinctive characteristic. By conveying the expressive, self-giving character of the biblical Lord, beauty opens us to enjoy God.

1. *Approaching Beauty*

The next four paragraphs are the famous first chapter of *Cry, the Beloved Country,* a novel of South Africa by Alan Paton. Even though the scene is unfamiliar, the language conveys beauty and, through beauty, meaning. You may enhance the passage if you read Paton's words aloud or ask a friend to read them to you.

There is a lovely road that runs from Ixopo into the hills. These hills are grass-covered and rolling, and they are lovely beyond any singing of it. The road climbs seven miles into them, to Carisbrooke; and from there, if there is no mist, you look down on one of the fairest valleys of Africa. About you there is grass and bracken and you may hear the forlorn crying of the titihoya, one of the birds of the veld. Below you is the valley of the Umzimkulu, on its journey from the Draneksburg to the sea; and beyond and behind the river, great hill after great hill; and beyond and behind them, the mountains of Ingeli and East Griqualand.

The grass is rich and matted, you cannot see the soil. It holds the rain and the mist, and they seep into the ground, feeding the streams in every kloof. It is well-tended, and not too many cattle feed upon it; not too many fires burn it, laying bare the soil. Stand unshod upon it, for the ground is holy, being even as it came from the Creator. Keep it, guard it, care for it, for it keeps men, guards men, cares for men. Destroy it and man is destroyed.

Where you stand the grass is rich and matted, you cannot see the soil. But the rich green hills break down. They fall to the valley below, and falling, change their nature. For they grow red and bare; they cannot hold the rain and mist, and the streams are dry in the kloofs. Too many cattle feed upon the grass, and too many fires have burned it. Stand shod upon it, for it is coarse and sharp, and the stones cut under the feet. It is not kept, or guarded, or cared for, it no longer keeps men, guards men, cares for men. The titihoya does not cry here any more.

The great red hills stand desolate, and the earth has torn away like flesh. The lightning flashes over them, the clouds pour down upon them, the dead streams come to life, full of the red blood of the earth. Down in the valleys women scratch the soil that is left, and the maize hardly reaches the height of a man. They are valleys of old men and old women, of mothers and children. The men are away, the young men and the girls are away. The soil cannot keep them any more.[1]

To communicate beauty, Alan Paton chooses measured, rhythmic language. The paragraphs are like a poem—perhaps more like a hymn, with verses and repetition. When Paton suggests he is "singing of it," he is correct: the language is lyrical.

Paton engages our sensory imagination. From a rising road our mind's eye is led to nearby hills covered with grass, then to the vista of a deep river valley flowing away from us, then to the great hills on the far side and the mountains beyond them. Our hearing, too, is summoned. We hear the "forlorn crying of the titihoya" in our mind's ear, even though we may never in fact have heard the cry of this strange bird. Then our sense of touch is beckoned, as we place bare feet upon the grass-matted soil, soft to the touch.

Having awakened our sensory imagination, Paton now stimulates other levels of imaginative experience. "The ground is holy." The word "holy" elicits a response of wonder, and we expect a revelation—that is, a new experience. Paton's image recalls Moses standing unshod before the burning bush, awaiting his word from the Lord. But here the revelation is the experience of the ground itself. "For the ground is holy, being even as it came from the Creator." In two short paragraphs, Paton leads us to the point where we grasp that the earth is sacred, and therefore it must be kept, and guarded, and cared for. He captivates us not by argument but by the quality of his images. He arouses our sensory imagination so that we might share his intuition.

Sensing that the ground is holy, we now enter in the realm of moral beauty, the beauty of truth. Paton describes physical ugliness to heighten our moral sense. He directs our mind's eye downward to land which is red, eroded, overgrazed, and burned; he pricks our senses with sharp stones, requiring us imaginatively to place our shoes upon our feet again. He asks us to listen here, in vain, for the titihoya.

The climactic image is one of the "holy" earth, bleeding like a living creature. My own imagination, nourished by the imagery of the Bible, calls up Isaiah's image of the "suffering servant"—the innocent victim of human tyranny whose suffering may yet redeem the abusers. Christians often apply this image to Jesus, but here Alan Paton seems to apply it to the earth itself.

The land bleeds because one group of people is oppressing another. The lowland dwellers are the Zulu people; they lived gently in this region before they were crowded into the most arid parts by the whites, whose flocks now graze the highlands. The Zulus have long loved the soil, though it can no longer keep them. The whites, well satisfied, now love the green hills which they have settled. But in spite of this love, much of the land is torn and bleeding from the whites' oppression of the Zulus.

Before any of this background unfolds, however, we have simply a vision of holy ground, beloved by its Creator, bleeding. The image Paton presents, stimulating us to notice a landscape and to ponder the human connections to it, is beautiful. This is what beauty does. It creates a relationship.

* * *

We use the word *beauty* to express a wide range of sensory and intellectual experiences. We may think first about visual images—the beauty of a sunset, a butterfly, a painting—but we know beauty just as well through our other four senses: the lilt of a song, the pleasing aroma from a rose, the sharp taste of a tart apple, the coolness of matted grass under our feet, the caress of a lover.

Beauty can also be an intellectual experience. A beautiful idea, for example, may be a fresh insight which promises to solve a problem or to overcome an obstacle. A beautiful idea may communicate the essence of a complex or mysterious relationship: the law of gravity, a theorem in geometry, a psychological insight, a prophetic moral statement.

It is the character of beauty to be engaging. The observer and the object seen as beautiful are not detached from each other; something is happening between them. When one dictionary distinguishes between *"beautiful, lovely, pretty, handsome, comely, fair "* it states:

> All these adjectives apply to that which appeals to the senses or mind. *Beautiful,* the most comprehensive, applies to what stirs a heightened response of the senses and of the mind on its highest level.[2]

This same dictionary begins the definition of *beauty* as: "A pleasing quality associated with harmony of form or color, excellence of craftsmanship, truthfulness, originality, or other, often unspecifiable property."[3] The notion of "a pleasing quality" is central to this definition. Beauty engages the beholder. It pleases; it "stirs a heightened response."

From Plato to the modern era, several philosophers have given the notion of beauty important roles in their systems of thought. "Without beauty, what would become of being?" wrote Plotinus, who revived Platonic thought in the third century A.D.[4] He saw in beauty the attractive force which held beings together. Immanuel Kant, the great eighteenth-century philosopher, believed that the perception of beauty was the foundation of the human capacity for judgment. Kant affirmed, "The fact that man is affected by the sheer beauty of nature proves that he is made for and fits into this world."[5] This thought would seem to provide a foundation for ethical relationships with nature. In fact, however, Kant undercut such ethics in two ways. First, he argued that only humans were suitable objects for moral concern. Then he followed the Platonic tradition of attributing a special characteristic to the human experience of beauty which distinguished it from other pleasurable experiences. Kant believed the enjoyment of beauty was a "disinterested delight."[6] This differs from my emphasis upon the engaged character of the experience of beauty, a difference I will return to in the next chapter.

Another eighteenth-century thinker, Jonathan Edwards, has suggested an understanding of beauty which can lead to ethical relationships with nature. In his reflection upon the Great Awakening, the religious revival he helped initiate, Edwards became convinced that the experience of beauty is the key to the encounter between God and persons, and, indeed, that it is fundamental to human motivation. From this point, Edwards was able to define just what kind of religious experience is truly experience of God.

I have drawn from Edwards' insights, and added my own, as I developed a Christian perspective on the relationship between persons and nature. Beauty is not a category from which to deduce ethical rules. Rather, the experience of beauty creates a relationship which itself motivates ethical behavior. As we appreciate the beauty of the natural world, we come to value all forms of life. Environmental ethics—the desire to discern them and the energy to apply them—spring from this engagement with natural beauty.

2. *Taste and See*

Beauty is engaging; it attracts attention. This observation about beauty can be expressed in either psychological or philosophical language. In psychological language, *the experience of beauty creates and sustains relationships.* I will consider shortly the fact that our experience of beauty is subjective, but here I wish to stress that beauty draws the observer toward the beautiful. In philosophical language, *beauty is an aspect of that which holds all things together.* It is a real characteristic of the world we know, a necessary quality of that world. If we diminish the world's beauty, we diminish the world's capacity to exist and ability to survive.

A striking feature of the natural world is how many things work together to support existence, each contributing to the life of others. We call this a *universe*: a whole composed of many interdependent and mutually supporting parts. If the many things in existence did not support each other, there would be *chaos* instead, in which most things attack, destroy, or flee from each other. We can easily imagine, for example, that following a nuclear war there might be such physical destruction, disruption of the ecosystem, and genetic mutation as to lead toward chaos and destroy the universe of life-support on this planet. The first verses of the Bible record an imagination of watery chaos existing before creation, before God's word shaped a stately development of life in a universe.

By contrast, when we look at the beauty of the natural world, we see that both the animate and inanimate tend to support each other. Each, directly or indirectly, contributes to the life of all. Equally striking is the amazing diversity which is so supported. The world's life-support system does not make everything the same, but rather permits the flowering of so many different things. From our perspective, the earth—with all its complexity of life and activity—is more beautiful than an alternative, sterile planet. We see that an important aspect of the beauty of the universe is the process of *individuation,* by which species become differentiated from one another; and by which individuals within species, sustained by interdependence, develop their unique potential.

Most of the beautiful relationships in the world happen naturally. That is, they do not appear to involve either consciousness or deliberate decisions. This is the beauty in the warp and woof of material existence, such as the intricate chemical interdependence of earth, air, and water which, activated by energy from the sun, yields living plants and creatures. These natural patterns of life support and individuation may also be present in our conscious, deliberate behavior when beauty enters our motivation. Indeed, awareness of beauty contributes to responsible behavior. If the sight of beauty arouses warm, positive feelings in us, we are motivated to a response which may add beauty to the relationship. Most of us find love, engaging and supportive, to be beautiful. If such love encourages the growth of another person into a distinctive self, it is even more beautiful.

Thus beauty is more than an accidental quality of the world. It is neither a decorative attribute nor a happy chance—but a necessity. Beauty has a positive attraction, leading us toward what is good for ourselves and for others. Because beauty reflects the health of life, its very absence can serve to warn us of problems: what we see may be damaged, or our relationship to it may be disoriented.

* * *

Initially we experience beauty in the relationships which nourish us, and we respond to that beauty just as we respond to nourishment. Here is the truth in the aphorism "Beauty is a matter of taste." The human reception of beauty is like our sense of taste. With taste—more than with hearing, sight, or touch—we must open our bodies and take in what we wish to experience. Taste, therefore, requires a particular openness. If we fear, we will refuse to taste; if we are forced, the taste will be unpleasant.

Jonathan Edwards often associated beauty with the sense of taste, as when he said, "The beauty and sweetness of the objects draws on the faculties." Indeed Edwards used the image of "sweetness" so often that a modern reader might think him saccharine or cloying. But when Edwards referred to the "loveliness and sweetness . . . of the Divine nature," he was stressing God's availability to human experience.[1] With this same sense the psalmist invited us to "taste and see that the Lord is good." (Psalm 34:8, KJV).

Since taste requires openness, we will not see beauty in what we fear. It will be ugly. When the Pilgrims first reached Cape Cod, they were too tempest-tossed to see the beauty in the land they had desired. William Bradford could characterize the scene he beheld only as "a hidious and desolate wilderness, full of wild beasts and wild men."[2]   Fear tends to screen positive experience and to block warm emotions. In appreciating natural beauty, humans often prefer the domesticated to the wild; it is under control and less threatening. For our sense of beauty to function as a guide to ethics, we must first overcome our fears.

The experience of beauty also resembles the experience of taste in that response to pleasure—or distaste—is immediate. We may choose to reflect upon sights or sounds, and such reflection may change the quality of the experience for us. Taste, however, is not usually a matter for reflection.[3] In psychological terms, the experience of beauty is an *immediate intuition*—an indirect perception by way of the unconscious. In the experience of beauty, sensory data combine with memories, desires, and other associations drawn from unconscious levels of our mind, so that our conscious perception is enriched. Edwards said that what we call beautiful is "immediately pleasant to the mind." We do not discover beauty through reasoning, comparison, or analysis, he said, "any more than tasting the sweetness of honey, or perceiving the harmony of a tune, is by argumentation on connections and consequences."[4]

We know beauty subjectively. We each find beauty from our unique point-of-view, because the experience of beauty is personal, emotional involvement. Is Mozart's "Piano Concerto No. 21 in C Major" beautiful? Many people feel that it is. But it is not beautiful for me until that day when I hear it and it moves me: when my mind and my feelings join in the music and move along with it. One cannot prove the beauty of Mozart's composition in a way that separates it from personal experience. To attempt some rational-aesthetic proof would be to bypass the beauty of music, beauty which exists in our hearing and responding. Theologian Karl Barth expresses this relational quality of aesthetic judgment in an imaginative "Letter of Thanks to Mozart":

> Whether the angels play only Bach in praising God I am not quite sure; I am sure, however, that *en famille* they play Mozart and that then also God the Lord is especially delighted to listen to them.[5]

Our experience of beauty begins with the gratifying, nurturing tastes of infancy. In the process of maturing, however, we extend our sense of beauty beyond immediate gratification. We develop imagination and empathy, learning to see beauty in things which do not so directly affect us. As we experience their beauty we become vulnerable to them; we acquire a stake in the existence of that which is beautiful. Because its loss would affect us, we are motivated to protect its life or continuance. The experience of beauty—by a remote wilderness lake in Idaho, or in a cathedral in France—tends to create a moral relationship. It now matters if the wilderness is threatened by oil drilling, or if the cathedral is vulnerable to warfare. Moral concern and ethical sensitivity do not grow from disinterestedness, but from affectionate engagement with the distinctive qualities of another being.

We can now see how far this understanding of beauty differs from Kant's. Kant believed that the enjoyment of beauty could be distinguished from other human experience in that such enjoyment was "disinterested delight." In the understanding I have developed from Edwards, however, the essence of the experience of beauty is not disinterest, but engagement. Beauty is an attraction which draws us to another and establishes a deeper interdependence.

Kant based his analysis on traditional *faculty psychology*, which distinguishes the faculty of reason from those of will and affections, and which exalts reason to the highest seat in the soul. He sought to protect reason from undue influence by the lower faculties. Unknown to Kant, across the Atlantic Jonathan Edwards had already replaced this faculty psychology with insight that anticipated modern perspectives. Edwards understood that emotional relationships are at the core of the human psyche: "The affections of men are the springs of the motion," of all human activity. In his brilliant treatise *Freedom of the Will*, Edwards argued that the will is brought into existence as we are drawn affectionately toward an object of delight. It is hardly an independent faculty. Edwards also argued that the full exercise of reason depends upon emotional engagement. He found "sensible knowledge," which drew energy and insight from emotional engagement, to be far superior to "mere speculative knowledge."[6] Beauty, in particular, stimulates the intellectual faculty.

> It engages the attention of the mind. . . . The beauty and sweetness of the objects draws on the faculties, and draws forth their exercises; so that reason itself is under far greater advantages for its proper and free exercises, and to attain its proper end, free of darkness and delusion.[7]

John Muir, America's seminal environmentalist, would make precisely the same point 250 years later. If the observer of nature could "become all eye, sifted through and through with light and beauty," the "inexpressible delight" which resulted would also motivate sound learning:

> The influences of pure nature seem to be so little

known as yet, that it is generally supposed that complete pleasure of this kind, permeating one's very flesh and bones, unfits the student for scientific pursuits in which cool judgment and observation are required. But the effect is just the opposite. Instead of producing a dissipated condition, the mind is fertilized and stimulated and developed like sun-fed plants.[8]

In Immanuel Kant's system, beauty, as "disinterested delight," supported judgment. Judgment was the function of the spectator, the philosopher. This was the highest human calling. Kant believed that the goal of nature was to produce, in the human species, some who could reflect disinterestedly upon the beauty of life and thus judge the quality of both nature and history.

For Edwards, beauty engaged the affections. As it stimulated will, thought, and action, beauty created relationships. Unlike Kant, Edwards believed that the goal of human life was affectionate engagement with all existence, particularly with God, who is supremely beautiful. Loving, not reflection, was the highest human vocation. While love for God was primary, all that was beautiful, all that could be loved, was drawn into the moral realm. I join Edwards in believing that humans are not destined to be spectators. We carry, in the image of God, responsibility for life in the world. We have a vocation both to experience and to cultivate the beauty of the world.

*   *   *

Our relation to beauty is subjective, for we encounter beauty in the particular relationships of our lives. This experience of beauty is real, but corruptible. The selfish person grasping the relationships that bring personal satisfaction and security builds walls against those aspects of the world which appear threatening and may ignore most of the world altogether. "We are apt, through the narrowness of our views, in judging of the beauty of affections and actions," Edwards observed, "to limit our consideration to only a small part of the created system."[9] A more open person, however, may be drawn outward by the experience of beauty to explore its broader connections. We all begin with particular beauties, since human perceptions of beauty are personal and personally involving, bound by our own time, place, and other limiting characteristics. Edwards believed it was God's grace that helped some expand their experiences, interrelating particular perceptions into more inclusive perspectives, seeing new beauties of a broader character. He attributed to virtue what I would call an ecological dimension: "The nature of true virtue consists in a disposition to benevolence towards being in general."[10] For Edwards, the most comprehensive vision of beauty reveals the beauty of God.

Note, however, that the distinction between our perception of particular beauties and our perception of more general beauties is not a distinction between the sensory, on the one hand, and the more rational or dispassionate, on the other. Broader perspectives may require more intellectual effort. All perceptions of beauty, however, have an emotional, engaging quality. The distinction is simply between the narrowness and the relative breadth or complexity of what is perceived.

A broad perception of beauty may revise a perception of particular beauty. We may encounter a New England lake, stunning in its absolute clarity. Its beauty is engaging. However, we may discover that the clarity of this lake results from acid rain pollution which has killed all the life in the lake, and which threatens the life systems in the region. If we find complex life more beautiful, and care enough to work to restore complex ecosystems, we may seek changes which diminish the visual clarity of this lake but which return to it the beauty of life.

Though our perceptions are subjective, beauty remains a real, essential quality of our universe. My particular perception of beauty may be distorted, though no perception that draws me toward another is completely wrong. Beauty exists so long as we continue in an interdependent, life-giving world, so long as there are beings with supportive relationships among them. Such supportive relationships exist between the fish and the ocean, between the proton and the electron, between wood and fire—and they are beautiful. There are also conscious, engaged relationships between God and persons, between one person and another, between the craftsperson and the material to be wrought—and these relationships, in their deliberate interaction, are particularly beautiful to us.

3. *Ecology*

The science and technology that have shaped the modern world do not value beauty as I have. Science may indeed uncover beauty, as it reveals affecting aspects of the world. Technology may create beauty, suggesting elegant solutions to complex problems, and creating tools that facilitate human engagement with life. Yet our dominant tradition of science and technology has generally not affirmed a sensuous and moral engagement with life—the style implied by awareness of beauty as I have defined it. Modern science is based on a dispassionate attitude, a detachment from emotional involvement with the materials of life; modern technology is manipulative. In the seventeenth century Francis Bacon set the task for both with his aphorism "Knowledge is Power." The intention of both science and technology has been to manipulate and to control the substance of the earth for human ends—to extend, in Bacon's words, "the empire of man over things."[1]

This approach has transformed the face of the earth. All things, whether living or inanimate, are now exposed to human technology and vulnerable to human manipulation. Although we have built a better life for many people, side effects of our knowledge and power have been damaging. Sometimes eagerly, sometimes ignorantly, sometimes carelessly, we have inflicted many wounds upon the earth. Now human society so dominates the earth's surface that the life and health of most living things must depend on human wisdom, sensitivity, restraint, and good will. Tragically, such self-restraint, respect for other forms of life, and compassion for needs other than human ones are not values honored within our dominant technological tradition.

However, as the impact of human society upon the life of the world has grown so alarmingly during the twentieth century, an alternative scientific perspective has emerged. Some have begun to study the relationships between things, motivated by a desire to avoid damage to natural systems, the supports for human life. The science of ecology, defined as "the science of the organism in relation to its environment and of the relations between communities of organisms of like or different kinds,"[2] is a significant part of this new perspective. Ecologists cultivate understanding of both the interrelationships among forms of life, and of the relationships between life forms and the sun, air, water, and earth which sustain life.

Not all ecologists exhibit a new perspective. There are academic ecologists who continue the traditional dispassionate, manipulative approach in their science, analyzing interspecies energy budgets, for example, in order to stimulate production. The more visible group of ecological scientists, however, have developed a refreshing point of view.[3] Many modify, with humility, the manipulative arrogance which has so often characterized modern science. Some, such as ecologists Dillon Ripley and Helmut Buechner, even see limits to the human capacity to understand:

> Ecosystems at the highest level of biological integration are not only more complex than we think they are, but more complex than we *can* think. Thus, we can never achieve a total understanding of the human society-plus-environment system.[4]

The dominant scientific tradition cultivated emotional detachment from the material under investigation. In addition, scientists often claimed their methods were value free, a claim which protected them from having to cope with the implications of underlying, but unacknowledged, beliefs and assumptions. It is remarkable, therefore, that many ecologists now acknowledge their values and express their feelings within their discipline. Aldo Leopold, founder of modern wildlife management, expressed his values forthrightly. "When we see land as a community to which we belong," he wrote, "we may begin to use it with love and respect. There is no other way for land to survive the impact of mechanized man, nor for us to reap from it the esthetic harvest it is capable, under science, of contributing to culture."[5]

By the end of the 1960s, at the dawning of the era of environmental activism, ecologists in the Leopold tradition were aware that their perspective posed a direct challenge to technological trends in Western society. Some, like Paul Shepard, saw themselves participating in a "subversive science":

> The ideological status of ecology is that of a resistance movement. Its Rachel Carsons and Aldo Leopolds . . . challenge the public or private right to pollute the environment, to systematically destroy predatory animals, to spread chemical pesticides indiscriminately, to meddle chemically with food and water, to appropriate without hindrance space and surface for technological and military ends; they oppose the uninhibited growth of human populations, . . . the extinction of species of plants and animals, the domestication of all wild places, large-scale manipulation of the atmosphere or the sea, and most other purely engineering . . . intrusions into the organic world.[6]

The ecological perspective has an affinity to the understanding of beauty which I have suggested. As practiced in affectionate regard for nature, *ecology may be a science interpreting the beauty of the earth*, or a science of natural beauty. Ecology is a modern science which may develop understanding of the relationships among beings in the natural order. The application of such ecological insight to public policy is a moral imperative if humanity is to care for the earth so that it, and we, may survive.

So I substitute this ecological perspective for the Platonism which has characterized philosophies of beauty developed by Kant and Edwards, as well as nineteenth-century American Transcendentalists. Platonic lovers of natural beauty justified their regard for nature by drawing from nature implications for higher truth; their values were not shaped by the threats to nature's continuance that color modern attitudes. We who are anxious that the earth survive can, without apology, focus our love on nature itself and attend to the beauty within natural relationships.

* * *

Ecological analysis can expand our awareness of beauty by helping us understand environmental systems and appreciate their value. Human life and welfare depend upon the healthy function of such systems. Many of these systems are threatened by pollution which may result from our affluent consumption patterns, our modern technologies, or our growing population. When we become conscious of environmental systems, we can appreciate their distinctive beauties. Becoming aware of threats to the environment arouses our feelings, and such emotional engagement makes it possible to see the beauty of nature more deeply; beauty is not a detached perception. This ecological understanding of natural beauty also heightens our sensitivity to ugliness, as when we view a polluted stream with understanding of its consequences. Ugliness is not the opposite of beauty; it is the companion of tasting beauty in this world. The true opposite of beauty is a dullness or insensibility to the world around us. Since the perception of beauty grows from engagement, it may be stimulated by knowledge of our interdependence. With nature, as with a personal friend, we may need to feel a threat of loss to awaken love that is appropriately intense—love that is strong enough to motivate both reflection and action.

This ecological perspective also helps us appreciate the beauty in some aspects of natural life that our culture has taught us to fear or find distasteful. By showing how species sustain each other even as they consume each other, ecological analysis reveals the beauties within the "eat-and-be-eaten" system that is the essence of life-support on this planet. It may not be a beautiful experience for a human observer to witness a wolf bring down a weakened deer at the end of winter, but ecological analysis shows how such events most often serve not only the wolves, but the general welfare of the natural system, and even the deer population itself.

Such is the principal lesson Aldo Leopold learned in a lifetime study of wildlife. He began his career as an eager manipulator of the natural environment, promoting the elimination of predators in order to increase deer herds for hunting and to protect domestic livestock; later he learned that predators are essential to a healthy, wild ecosystem. He wished he had been more patient and attentive to the lessons of nature. "Only the mountain has lived long enough to listen objectively to the howl of a wolf," he wrote.

> . . . I have lived to see state after state extirpate its wolves. I have watched the face of many a newly wolfless mountain, and seen the south-facing slopes wrinkle with a maze of new deer trails. I have seen every edible bush and seedling browsed, first to anaemic desuetude, and then to death. I have seen every edible tree defoliated to the height of a saddle-horn. . . . In the end the starved bones of the hoped-for deer herd, dead of its own too-much, bleach with the bones of the dead sage, or molder under the high-lined junipers.[7]

Reflecting on the human prejudice against our fellow predators, wildlife ecologist Durward Allen suggests that an "impartial sympathy toward *all* creatures, regardless of their diet" should become "an attitude of the cultivated mind":

> It is a measure of a man's civilization. If ever we are to achieve a reasonable concord with the Earth on which we live, it will be by our willingness to recognize, tolerate, and employ the biological forces and relationships both in our own numbers and in the living things about us.[8]

At age thirteen, just before he entered Yale College, the precocious Jonathan Edwards wrote a treatise on spiders which showed amazing gifts of natural observation. He concluded by expressing admiration for the divine ecology that balanced spiders' vulnerability to drowning and predation with their high birthrate.

> Admire also the Creator in so nicely and mathematically adjusting their Multiplying nature that Notwithstanding their Destruction by this means and the Multitudes that are eaten by birds that they Do not Decrease and so by little and little come to nothing, and in so adjusting their Destruction to their multiplication that they Do neither increase but taking one year with another there is alwaies Just an equal number Of them.[9]

We humans depend upon the food chain for our sustenance. I believe it would enhance our emotional health, and also encourage more ethical relationships with nature, if we learned to overcome the fearful alienation that keeps us from understanding death as a part of the beauty of life on this planet. Life on this earth depends on death. Fear of death inhibits our appreciation of life—our own life, and other natural life.

Farming has given me an opportunity to raise and to care for plants and animals. Part of farming is harvesting and slaughter, so that people may be fed and more crops may be grown. Although there are ethical dilemmas in this role which need to be pondered carefully, I can see beauty in this cycle. I wish to grow in my ability to care sensitively for the life on Chestnut Ridge Farm, including plants grown for consumption and animals raised for slaughter. Furthermore, my experience with farming has helped me think more constructively about death. I look toward my own death with greater equanimity. On a crowded planet, it will be good finally to step aside so another may enjoy the world I have known. I know where I wish to be buried, beneath a favorite sugar maple. To me it is important that my body be in a plain wooden box without protective vault, so it will rot to nourish other life, joining the beautiful cycle of renewal.

*   *   *

My ecological perspective on the beauty of the earth informs my philosophical understanding of beauty as a necessary reality. Creative interrelationships between forms of life, matter, and energy are essential for the maintenance of life on this planet. That is to say, the beauty of the world is essential to the survival of the world. If we disrupt these beautiful relationships so that support is replaced by destructive contact—so that the air carries poison to plants rather than nourishment—we will begin to destroy life itself. As Plotinus observed, "Without beauty, what would become of being?" Beauty, while always subjectively perceived, is not just a matter of opinion. It is a characteristic of healthy relationships between beings. Within the ecosystem, when beings support the lives of other beings, then beauty is present. When beings damage the fabric of life, however, these actions are ugly and weaken the universe.

In Platonic reflection, the perception of beauty lifted the mind away from material reality to the world of ideas where beauty could be known rationally. The concepts of "form" and "proportion" assisted this rational comprehension of beauty. However, from the ecological perspective, form and proportion are less significant contributors to the experience of beauty. Instead of using these classic terms, I suggest that natural beauty is experienced primarily through the *interplay of interdependence with individuality*.

In the organic world, our first school of beauty, we see that each specific animal, plant, leaf, flower, or snowflake is distinctive. Symmetry is rarely perfect, even in the petals of a rose. The shape of a particular tree is the product of complex interaction between the genetic energy of the tree, the health of the soil, the slope of the terrain, the direction of the sun and prevailing winds, crowding from other trees, and events in the tree's history such as lightning or drought. If we are able to relate to a tree as a living being, we will see the beauty expressed in a triumphant interaction with these forces, even though the tree may be leaning out from the south edge of the woods or standing gnarled from many battles with the elements. The form derives from a unique interaction between the tree's genetic nature, its aliveness, and its particular environment. When we limit a tree to being a mere decorative backdrop for human activity, classic form and symmetry may become dominant criteria in our perception of its beauty.

The ecological perspective on beauty alerts us to the importance of diversity. The more diverse a particular ecosystem is, the more stable and healthy it is likely to be; the greater the variety of species within the system, the more resistant the system is to blight or attack, and the more resources it has to recover from attack. Thus the capacity for mutual support, widely considered and over the long term, is increased in proportion to the diversity of the ecosystem. Life is best supported by diversity. Beauty is manifest in this diversity, both in the complexity of the whole and in the uniqueness of each life.

I apply this understanding to human culture. Some have believed that social health depends upon how similar the members of a society are to each other, and how much they agree. These thinkers seek social peace through social conformity. All totalitarian societies, on the left and right, implement this bias. From an ecological perspective, however, it is the diversity of talents, personalities, views, and gifts within the human population, along with the diversity of subcultures within a society, which gives the best hope to meet the unpredictable vicissitudes of social history. Diversities in open warfare with each other can, of course, damage or destroy a society. But as long as a society can accommodate diversities within a functioning social system, it is accommodating the resources that support its survival and stimulate its creativity. I find such a society beautiful. (I realize, however, that explaining human culture with analogies drawn from nature, or explaining nature with analogies drawn from our culture, is not always appropriate, and that each analogy of this type needs to be evaluated on its merits.)

If beauty exists when beings support the life and

individuality of each other, then moral beauty occurs when there is conscious choice to do so, when beauty stimulates a deliberate, affectionate engagement by a conscious agent. We enter such moral relationships step by step. An appreciation of beauty may start with the desire to "bag" a moose and hang its wonderful head on the wall, then expand to a desire to protect the range that moose need for survival, then expand through further experience into appreciation for the whole complex ecosystem of which moose are a part. If moose are scarce, the lover of beauty may come to prefer leaving the moose on the range.

I add a further consideration: *the beauty in life-giving, affectionate relationships is heightened when such affection recognizes diversity, supports individuality, or spans distinctions between beings.* Here we may think of the love that does not wish to make the other "just like me," but is eager to help the other thrive. Or we may think of beautiful acts that reach across barriers of hatred and distrust, like the surprising visit of Egypt's President Anwar Sadat to Israel, which began the process leading to a peace treaty. Christian piety has portrayed as most beautiful the redeeming relationship between the righteous God and sinful persons; the moral gulf between them dramatizes the beauty of transcending this distance in Christ.

For society to learn to care for the earth rather than destroy it, human beings must empathically span the distinctions between human life and other forms of life, and indeed between reflective life and all forms of matter and energy. Where this happens, when persons learn to care for animals, plants, land, and water in ways that support their diversity and life-giving interactions, the results are beautiful.

4. *The Beauty of the Lord*

"God is God, and distinguished from all other beings, and exalted above 'em, chiefly by his divine beauty." [1] Among Christian philosophers and theologians, Jonathan Edwards is unique, I believe, in suggesting that beauty is God's most distinctive characteristic.

Western philosophy has employed rational disciplines developed by Plato, Aristotle, and other ancient Greek thinkers. These disciplines differ from the more engaging, but less analytic, biblical style of reflection. When Christian philosophers have thought analytically about the biblical Lord, they have attributed to God perfections derived from the Greek style of categorical analysis: God is considered to be immortal, changeless, omnipotent, self-subsistent, unmovable, and so forth. Philosophical theologians also use rational analysis to interpret characteristics suggested more directly by the biblical tradition: God's wisdom, word, and spirit; God's justice, love, and truth.

In the Bible itself, however, there is more emphasis on God's active engagement with humanity and the world. The Bible celebrates God's creativity rather than defining God as Creator. The biblical Lord has personality that is not constrained by some list of desirable characteristics. God loves, God becomes angry, God expresses moral indignation, God repents. Some of this behavior rests uncomfortably with Greek notions of perfections appropriate to God. Yet Christians are committed to knowing God through personality. We believe that God is revealed most completely not in abstract categories or even in cosmic acts, but in a particular man Jesus who taught, healed, loved, wept, became angry, suffered, and even died.

The static categories used by theologians have often been inadequate to express the dynamic character of the biblical God they were writing about. Jonathan Edwards did not abandon traditional categories, but by selecting beauty as central, he breathed life into his systematic reflection. Beauty, for Edwards, was far more than a rational category: it was an experience. Indeed, beauty was at the core of the experience that opens persons to God.

As we have seen, beauty is not a quality in isolation, but is realized in relationships. Therefore, when affirming that "God is distinguished . . . chiefly by his divine beauty," Edwards was saying that God's fundamental characteristic is active involvement with other beings. Creation, love, governance, and redemption are not activities incidental to the character of God. They express the very heart of who God is.

The Bible attributes beauty to God, but this quality is not mentioned nearly so often as God's love, or justice, or goodness. Where the Bible does ascribe beauty to God, however, the idea is compatible with the significance Edwards proposed. Psalm 27 (RSV, alt.) illustrates how God's beauty may be understood biblically. The Psalm is attributed to David, who began with an affirmation that the Lord shines forth, that God is not self-absorbed or removed.

> The Lord is my light and my salvation;
>   whom shall I fear? (vs. 1)

As he drew closer to the Lord, David expressed his desire for a vision of God. He wanted to see God's "beauty":[2]

> One thing have I asked of the Lord,
>   that will I seek after;
> that I may dwell in the house of the Lord
>   all the days of my life,
> to behold the beauty of the Lord,
>   and to inquire in [God's] temple. (vs. 4)

Twice again in his poem David expressed hope for this
vision. In these instances he used words more common to the
Bible: the "face" of God in one, the "goodness" of God in another.

> Hear, O Lord, when I cry aloud,
>> be gracious to me and answer me!
> Thou hast said, "seek ye my face."
>> My heart says to thee,
> "Thy face, Lord, do I seek."
>> Hide not thy face from me. (vss. 7–9)

> I believe that I shall see the goodness of the Lord
>> in the land of the living!
> Wait for the Lord:
>> be strong, and let your heart take courage;
>> yea, wait for the Lord! (vss. 13–14)

"Beauty," "goodness," and "face" were used equiva-
lently. "Goodness" was always central to the biblical understanding of God. The "Face," characteristically hidden, was a
common biblical expression for the essence of the Lord's personality. David selected the image of beauty as another way
of expressing a full and intimate relation to God.

Beauty was also used by Isaiah as a poetic equivalent
to other common terms for God's self-expression. Imagining a
time of restoration, when Israel would have direct communion with the Lord, Isaiah equated God's glory with God's
beauty, and paired them with God's justice and strength.

> In that day the Lord of hosts will be a crown of *glory*,
>> and a diadem of *beauty*, to the remnant of his people;
> and a spirit of *justice* to him who sits in judgment,
>> and *strength* to those who turn back the battle at the
>>   gate.   (Isaiah 28:5–6 RSV, emphasis added)

Like Edwards, I choose beauty as my central theological image. I find it especially useful for opening Christian
experience to nature. By making this selection, however, I do
not mean to imply that Christian theologies are any less
legitimate if they take as central image God's goodness, God's

justice, God's love, God's glory, God's face, or God's word. In other contexts, any of these might appropriately serve as an integrating theme. Many words and images point to God's personality, but none limits our Lord.

One image I deliberately refrain from imposing upon God, however, is gender. Although human sexuality is at the core of our expressiveness and creativity, and the biblical Lord is more expressive still, biblical writers understood that the Hebrew God was not sexual in the sense of requiring or desiring a consort. This Lord does not need to couple with another for creativity. Therefore I do not use masculine or feminine pronouns with reference to God. To modern readers sensitive to equal rights and sexual imagery, these pronouns carry a connotation of actual gender which they may not have had in prior centuries. When I quote Edwards and other writers I do not change their use of pronouns, but I alter biblical versions when I believe the pronoun misleads.[3]

* * *

Beauty shows itself; it shines forth, eager to be seen and known. Similarly, God's perfection does not imply isolation or self-absorption. As Edwards argued, the perfection of God is inherently giving and creative. Edwards had a particular fondness for the Holy Spirit because the image of Spirit expresses this self-giving character of the Lord.

> It was made especially the Holy Spirit's work to bring the world to its beauty and perfection out of the chaos; for the beauty of the world is a communication of God's beauty. The Holy Spirit is the harmony and excellency and beauty of the deity. Therefore, 'twas His work to communicate beauty and harmony to the world, and so we read that it was He that moved upon the face of the waters. [4]

Reaching out is not a compromise or condescension from God's perfection; rather, it is the essence of the Lord's beauty. And God does not reach out in order to receive, but in order to shine forth. "The glory of God is the shining forth of His perfections. The world was created that they might shine forth—that is, that they might be communicated."[5] Not only is God manifest beautifully, but as Edwards affirmed again and again, "God delights in communicating his happiness to the creature."[6] God enjoys shining.

The sight of beauty arouses delight, and the experience of beauty is sensuous and emotional. When we know God, the Lord becomes an occasion for enjoyment which opens us to growth and change, shaping who we are and influencing how we live. In 1648 Edwards' Puritan ancestors expressed these relationships in the striking question and answer which open the Westminster Shorter Catechism:

> Q. 1. What is the chief end of man?
> A. Man's chief end is to glorify God, and to enjoy him forever.

As God's beauty creates our joy, so does our joy proclaim God's beauty.

Part II.

Landscapes of the Mind

When we look at a landscape we see more than what is there, and less also. If we are afraid, our perception may be blocked or distorted, and we see little to which we can relate. When we perceive beauty, however, we engage the landscape creatively: we order, we highlight, we find meaning. The mind is more than a photographic plate; the sight that gives insight differs from the camera image.

Lisel Mueller conveys this truth by imagining the impressionist painter Claude Monet remonstrating with an ophthalmologist who wishes to "correct" his vision.

> Doctor, you say there are no haloes
> around the streetlights in Paris
> and what I see is an aberration
> caused by old age, an affliction.
> I tell you it has taken me all my life
> to arrive at the vision of gas lamps as angels,
> to soften and blur and finally banish
> the edges you regret I don't see,
> to learn that the line I call the horizon
> does not exist and sky and water,
> so long apart, are the same state of being.
> Fifty-four years before I could see
> Rouen cathedral is built
> of parallel shafts of sun,
> and now you want to restore
> my youthful errors: fixed
> notions of top and bottom,
> the illusion of three-dimensional space,

wisteria separate
from the bridge it covers.
What can I say to convince you
the Houses of Parliament dissolve
night after night to become
the fluid dream of the Thames?
I will not return to a universe
of objects that don't know each other. . . [1]

Nature is vulnerable to the ways we see it. Healthy natural systems now depend both upon good human sight and insight. Our psychic health or sickness, our social justice or oppression, impact the earth. Frustrated people kick their dogs, while desperate farmers plow steep hillsides and allow their cattle to overgraze pastures. In exploitative societies, the most abused class is nature itself. Landscapes of the mind shape the land. For illustration, I turn to the Grand Canyon, for I could open my eyes to experience this awesome landscape only as I myself began to heal. From there I review how modern attitudes toward nature have been shaped by our personal projections and social values: scientific detachment; fear of strong feelings and shame at bodily desires; greed, class, and economic desperation. Even Darwin's biology, the foundation of modern ecology, was colored by projection of cultural anxieties.

This section proposes an image of human health rooted in the expressive integrity Jesus recommended. It uses Jonathan Edwards' psychology to bridge between traditional Christian themes and modern therapeutic insights. Edwards' emphasis on the critical importance of human affections resonates with Jesus' condemnation of insensibility, and also with modern psychotherapeutic insights which encourage us to express our capacities and engage with life. I hear from Jesus, from Edwards, and from modern healers a call to see and feel the world, to enjoy God, and to find ourselves.

5. *The Grand Canyon*

I made my fifth visit to the Grand Canyon in February 1986. This chapter contains my reflections during that week's stay. I have learned that my ability to experience natural beauty depends upon my wholeness: my physical vitality, emotional health, and spiritual openness. Landscapes can be threatening until we know ourselves.

*   *   *

Monday. Arriving yesterday at the south rim after dark, I rose before dawn this morning to watch the first light from the southeast dip into the canyon. Rocky old friends gently emerged. When the sun rose distant cliffs were etched in yellow light and deep shadows.

I first saw Grand Canyon in the summer of 1947, at age twelve. Mother, a woman companion from England, and I were driving our new Studebaker on the return portion of my first trip across America. I stared constantly out the window, never tiring of the cornfields, the desert plateaus, the rocky coast of California. Mother, who had visited Grand Canyon many times in her youth, anticipated it as the scenic climax of our trip.

For me, though, it was not. Standing at the rim overlook I could not comprehend the scene. It was far too vast, too overwhelming. Since Mother's excitement was mixed with an anxious acrophobia, her fear of heights, I was collared, warned, and supervised. Her friend expressed delight through photo after photo, some with me in the foreground, some with me behind the camera. After stops at four or five overlooks, I was eager to drive away. The gentler beauty of the painted desert calmed me.

This afternoon I walked along four miles of rim trail west of Canyon Village. Looking across the canyon I could see old friends: Bright Angel Canyon where Anne and I had walked to Ribbon Falls enjoying the honeymoon of our present marriage; Zoroaster Temple, a rock formation I had come to know the first time I hiked into the canyon, walking beneath it for hours which seemed endless under a blazing sun. I enjoyed gazing across the canyon to these forms, familiar in memory, until the rim trail led me to fresh vistas of unfamiliar canyons and cliffs which were now introduced to me, it seemed, by my old friends. I began to relish them.

A hundred feet below me on the steep side of the canyon, four mountain goats were nibbling bushes. They paid no attention to me, secure in their protective park. People came from their cars to stand behind me or beside me, taking pictures and exclaiming to each other at the views, but I was relaxed in my own meditations. The people did not disturb me. I was glad they were enjoying my friends.

*   *   *

Tuesday. I drove to where I had ended yesterday and continued on foot my exploration of the canyon rim.

Another memory surfaced: my second visit to the Grand Canyon, when I was thirty. That time I was the guide, and I planned everything carefully. It was early in my first marriage; my wife and two young sons were with me on their first driving trip to the west coast. We were enjoying the vacation.

(I feel the anxiety. It is difficult to write this down.) After we had settled into our cabin, I drove my family along the west rim in the evening light, stopping at several of the viewpoints where the canyon falls off abruptly, dropping thousands of feet into the chasm. Later, in bed, I confessed to my wife that I had fought back the urge to drive us over the precipice. I was afraid, and my confession scared her as well.

Through the night we held each other close. The next day I was fine.

I remember that confession, but it is harder to remember the feeling itself. It was quickly buried in those deep inner canyons of the mind where we hide those urges we do not want to face. Now I see it as a fissure in the ground of my apparently happy life, revealing for a moment a chasm of desperation. It was my first moment of panic, but not my last.

My rim-walk this morning extended beyond the trails constructed by the Park Service. I left them to follow the smaller footpaths, worn by many eager sightseers. Along the rim above the sheer Hopi Wall were places where the informal trail looked insecure. It was a mere path worn on the soft, wet ground that sloped sharply to the nearby lip of the chasm, and I began to follow it, simply because it was there. Then I realized I did not want to slide and die, nor did I want to watch the path every step and miss the vista. I climbed up higher and found footing that was more secure, if less exciting.

* * *

Wednesday. This morning I started down the Kaibab trail from the canyon rim to the Colorado River, seven miles with a drop of 4,800 feet. Happily most of the snow and ice from a storm two nights before had melted, even from the upper, shaded portions of the trail cut into the side of the rock cliff. I found it exhilarating to enter the canyon. The colors in the rock engaged me as never before. Just below the rim, the cliffs are predominantly yellow. Below those are red cliffs, folowed by the pale green of the Tonto Plateau, and finally the dark green-black granite of the inner gorge.

Today I noticed how pale the rock is when newly exposed by a break, and how complex the colors become as the rocks weather and age. I realized that the colors around me were alive. That is, they expressed energetic chemical and biological interactions as rock met sun, rain, and wind, as leaching metals interacted with the atmosphere, as lichen and plant life took hold, and as the whole system was caressed by cycles of sun, shadow, and darkness and challenged by heat, freezing, and thawing. The rock forms seemed stolid, but their colors were alive and active, producing an ever-changing array of hues to delight the eye. Reading John Muir prepared me for the notion that rocks speak their history, so a knowing eye can read an exciting story. But I have no geological training and can read little beyond the most crude outline. What I saw was the life of today—the colors rejoicing. In the Grand Canyon water and wind have rescued rocks from the dark depths of the earth and given them new birth in the light of day. They dress themselves in rich colors and give praise.

Halfway down I could look across the deep inner gorge where the Colorado River flowed, still hidden, and see clearly the Tonto Plateau above the north wall of the inner gorge, with Zoroaster Temple rising above it. With binoculars I could pick out portions of the trail I had walked thirteen years before.

My third visit to the Grand Canyon was in 1973. My marriage was collapsing, and earlier that year I had fled my home in the West Virginia coalfields and driven to Colorado in a desperate search for myself. After daily sessions with my psychotherapist I would hike in Boulder Mountain Park. Each day I walked a little farther or climbed a little higher until fatigue stopped me. This was my first attempt since childhood to cultivate a physical skill: a plump, dyslexic youngster, I had discovered that sports brought me ridicule. Now, however, learning to walk became the most significant part of my search. While my head wrestled uncertainly with anxious feelings and confused images from the past, my legs and lungs told me each day that I was getting a little stronger. When spring came I tried my first backpacking, overnight. Then a goal came clear to me—to hike into Grand Canyon. Following that, I could return to West Virginia to see if my marriage could be repaired.

At the last minute I persuaded a friend to accompany

me; I was anxious about making this descent alone. When we started down the steep Kaibab trail I walked close to her, chattering. After a couple of miles she suggested we walk separately so we could each have our own experience. We shared impressions when we stopped to rest.

The second day was the challenge. Joints aching and feet sore from the long descent, we left the campground by the Colorado River and climbed a trail up the north face of the inner gorge to the Tonto Plateau, which tilted toward the June sun. Our goal was Clear Creek, a camping spot with water, more distant than we had expected. Hot and sore under our heavy packs, we trudged across the desert landscape. Above us were the great stony arms of the Zoroaster Temple, like a huge, alien Sphinx. After walking the hot mile along the plateau, from beneath the first towering rock paw to beneath the second, we came to an identical landscape stretching toward a third paw, then a fourth, and even a fifth, before the day ended. About the seventh hour I doubted if I could continue, but after ten hours we finally crept to our camping spot and bathed our feet in the tiny lukewarm stream.

The next day we rested. As I gained strength, the great jutting cliffs began to appear beautiful. I felt distant from human culture and liberated from my anxieties. I was completely immersed in a wild landscape unlike any I had ever seen. Tired and sore, I was content simply to exist. For that day I felt at peace with myself and even with my surroundings, alien as they appeared. Despite lingering aches, the hike back and the climb out to the canyon rim were less difficult.

I returned to West Virginia but after three frustrating months, sunk to the bottom of despair and depression, I decided to abandon my struggle to rescue my marriage. Without the hike into the canyon, I would have been afraid to fall so far. Now, though, if I knew nothing else, I knew I could walk. The climb out to a new life took several years, but it was easier than going down.

Today I looked across the canyon to Zoroaster Temple
and picked out sections of the trail through my binoculars. I
thanked God for them. Does the temple know how much I
changed walking beneath it?

*   *   *

Thursday. No aches this morning from the descent to
the Colorado River. Though it was drizzling, I was eager to
hike north to Ribbon Falls. I walked along the deep gorge of
Bright Angel Creek. I could see where intermittent streams,
dry today, had polished the quartz and schist. These dry
streams of polished rock seemed to dance with the light of
memory, recalling rejoicing waters that tumbled down canyon
walls each spring to join Bright Angel Creek.

I had not noticed this the previous time I walked the
Bright Angel Canyon, but then I was preoccupied with Anne,
my new wife. We explored this side-canyon together on our
honeymoon. I wanted to share the Grand Canyon with her,
since it had become so meaningful to me. This was in 1975,
just two years after my more anxious descent, yet I was now
confident enough to lead a "tenderfoot" hiker into these beautiful depths.

On our third day in the canyon, hot and tired from
our exertions, we visited Ribbon Falls in its secluded amphi-
theater just off Bright Angel Creek. Remarkably, we were
alone. The delicate stream of limestone water poured down
from an extended lip of rock, falling fifty feet to strike a thirty-
foot-high stalagmite that it had created, then splashing down
the moss-covered sides of this giant green thumb to gather
again in a creek at the bottom. We shed our clothes and
climbed onto the stalagmite platform, high and happy as we
showered under the cool fall. Then we made love.

Now on this February morning more than a decade
later, the light rain ended as I walked the six miles to Ribbon
Falls, but the sky remained dull. Where I could glimpse the
distant, upper portions of the canyon toward the rim, the flat
surfaces were etched with new snow. A little hail fell as I
neared the falls.

However, as I walked into the rocky alcove that surrounds Ribbon Falls, the sun broke through for the first time. I climbed up against the rock cliff behind the falls and warmed myself in the sun as I watched the stream of water, heavier at this time of year, splash down upon the mossy stalagmite. The splash glistened in the sunlight. My tears came. They were not really about the Falls. They were for the joy Anne and I have known in the decade since we stood beneath this spray.

*   *   *

Friday. I sat on the Tonto Plateau beside the Clear Creek trail, below the spreading rock arms of Zoroaster Temple. Today's was an easy climb: no heavy pack, no heat, no anxiety. I thanked God for the rocks that towered over my struggles thirteen years ago.

*   *   *

Saturday. I was climbing out of the canyon, walking up another trail to the south rim. Six hundred feet below the rim I stopped to rest. It had been snowing for the past hour, and the trail and all flat surfaces were white. The yellow sandstone, too, was etched in white. The canyon itself was lost in cloud, visibility reduced to a small, wintry room.

Then the heaviest clouds began to lift from the canyon, rising to eye level. I could look down and see below a faint outline of a wooded refuge, "Indian Gardens," which I had walked through two hours before. Then parts of the green Tonto Plateau began to appear, surrounded by redstone walls, their colors muted. The scene was a romantic painting. Some reds and greens below me were highlighted in faint, distant sunlight, while mist surrounded and framed my view. Just above eye level, dark cloud strata hovered. Then snowflakes began to fall again, and the vision slowly melted away. I praised God for the living atmosphere. At last, like Monet, I had seen light.

6. *Projection*

Projection is the psychological term for attributing to another some characteristic—a feeling, idea, value, or the like—which is really one's own. Projection can be a constructive technique to help us engage with another; our projection of what another feels assists our interaction, while through continued exchange we confirm or modify the projection. Psychologically, however, the term most often describes one of the mechanisms we use to cloud our self-awareness. When we do not wish to acknowledge feelings deep within us, we may project those feelings onto others so we actually see them coming from another person. For example, if I am not able to admit my anger at my father, I may imagine he is angry with me.[1] Such disordered, confused projections play a large role in human attitudes toward the natural world. This chapter, and the next, examine modern projections that weaken our capacity to experience nature and confuse our attempts to relate responsibly to natural systems.

In Western culture, from biblical and Roman times to the modern industrial revolution, most people lived and worked closely with natural life. They farmed fields, hunted woods, and fished seas. Traders and the military depended upon horses and other draft animals for transport and power. Nature was an intimate companion—though, as with any forced intimacy, close relationships were not always cordial ones.

Taming the wilderness for human use, whether in medieval northern Europe or in the New World at the dawn of the modern era, was difficult and dangerous. Until the nineteenth century, beauty was appreciated in the ordered vistas of tended fields and domestic animals, while the wild landscape was generally regarded as ominous and ugly. Spanish explorers, looking for gold and Indian civilizations, first reached the rim of the Grand Canyon in 1540, but neither these nor any other adventurer who stumbled upon the canyon during the next three hundred years recorded any awe or delight. A Grand Canyon historian observed that "For Spain the Canyon was at best a hole, a vacuum of what was usable and assimilable, and at worst a disappointing barrier in the search for a maritime passage."[2] Not until the 1850s would the Grand Canyon be "discovered" as a wild, natural wonder.

Until the present century, urban people as well as rural ones depended upon animals to assist their labors. In northern Europe before the industrial era, the relationships between humans and animals were close indeed. During the cold months peasants often shared their rooms with their stock, to provide shelter for the animals and heat for the family. Urban areas crowded together people, horses, chickens, dogs, and many other creatures. Cities were noisy, smelly, polluted, diseased, and uncomfortable.

At the dawn of the modern era those with means were eager to improve their physical separation from animals, and intellectuals were likewise eager to distinguish the human from the animal. Human dependence upon animal power, as well as the discomforts of living closely with animals, may explain why early modern culture had more anxious concern for distinctions to separate humans from animals than seems reasonable to the people of the twentieth century, we who live apart from animals and feel secure in our dominance over the natural world.

The King James version of Psalm 8, translated in the early seventeenth century, seems to gloat over human dominion:

> Thou hast put all things under his feet:
> All sheep and oxen, yea, and the beasts of the field;
> The fowl of the air, and the fish of the sea . . .
> O LORD our Lord, how excellent . . . ! (vss. 6–9)

In the biblical tradition the relationships between humanity, animals, and natural life were more subtle and complex than Psalm 8 by itself suggests. Nature was understood to have its own responsive relationships with the Lord. Sabbath law constrained human abuse of domestic animals and gave some rights to plant life, to the land itself, and to wild animals, even in an agricultural setting. Human relations to nature, therefore, were seen as part of the moral structure of life. Indeed, the land was seen as responsive, not only to direct human care, but also to the quality of social justice: "If you walk in my statutes . . . the land shall yield its increase."[3] (Leviticus 26:3–4, RSV).

By the end of the Middle Ages, however, the Christian church's tenuous understanding of these moral relationships with nature had been lost. The mood of the Renaissance was better served by Aristotle's ancient affirmation that as everything had a purpose, so plants were created for the sake of animals, and animals for the sake of humanity.[4] This rational hierarchy appealed to the emerging practical mentality. The seventeenth-century father of modern science, Francis Bacon, believed that "Man . . . may be regarded as the centre of the world, insomuch that if man were taken away from the world, the rest would seem to be all astray, without aim or purpose."[5]

In that era of elaborate clocks and the first machines, scientific philosophers eagerly drew analogies between machines and biology. The French philosopher René Descartes argued that since animals lack a rational soul, they must function as automata like clocks, producing complex behavior without reflection, perhaps without sensation. Descartes believed the human body functioned the same way, though humanity, uniquely, joined reflective intellect to this clockwork. This "Cartesian" perspective was broadly influential. Some of Descartes' followers would reassure those engaged in early experiments that animals were in fact devoid of sensation: their howls and writhings were merely external reflexes, unconnected to any inner feelings.[6] In the development of science it was important to train people to assume a detached, "objective" posture toward other forms of life. Empathy, the projection that animals might feel as humans do, needed to be overcome.

The cultured were eager to separate themselves from the animal. To have others till one's land and care for one's stock was a sign of social position. A gentleman did not do these things for himself; nor did a lady hoe the garden, or kill and clean the goose for the table.

Medieval Christian theology had affirmed that humans have souls, a unique spiritual nature which separates them from animals.[7] The scientific disposition saw human uniqueness expressed in intelligence, the "rational soul." Both perspectives reinforced feelings of distance from other life and feelings of superiority to the animal. These spiritual and rational traditions shared a common weakness. They did not integrate feelings and desires—the emotional aspect of the human constitution—into their portrait of the human soul. People, especially those who were cultured, feared strong feelings.

It has been a Western trait to project onto the animal world those emotions we most fear in ourselves. Plato referred to "the wild beast within us" which might be curbed by religion and morality.[8] Identifying human emotions as "animal"—particularly those emotions which are strongly felt or which threaten to break the boundaries of social propriety—so pervades our culture that we scarcely notice it. As Oxford historian Keith Thomas observed, we have commonly labeled ferocity, gluttony, and sexuality as animal characteristics, "even though it was men, not beasts, who made war on their own species, ate more than was good for them and were sexually active all the year round. It was as a comment on *human* nature that the concept of 'animality' was devised."[9]

Thomas wrote a rich study of human attitudes toward nature in the early-modern, English speaking world: *Man and the Natural World, a History of Modern Sensibility.* He noted benefits to the privileged classes from projection of animal characteristics. If humanity was defined by certain intellectual and spiritual qualities, and if the less desirable human qualities were associated with animals, then those who lacked the preferred qualities, or manifested the undesired, might themselves be treated more like animals. Those who wished to clear America of "Indians" or to enslave African Negroes could stress how their appearance and behavior failed to reveal spiritual and intellectual qualities recognizable to the Western sensibility—how they manifested "animal" traits. This made it easier to subjugate Negroes as if they were domestic animals or to drive off American Indians as if they were wild beasts.

Likewise, the squalid poor coughed up by industrialization and urbanization could be considered beastlike and treated as such. An English nobleman wrote in 1693 that "The numerous rabble . . . are but brutes in their understanding. . . . At best they are but Descartes's automata, moving frames and figures of men."[10] Marginal persons, vagrants, and the mad could also be considered beastly. Here was a useful rationalization for social distinctions which could also justify harsh treatment or indifference to the welfare of the less fortunate.

Thomas showed how, in the early modern period, nature itself was seen through the eyes of social class. The care or abuse that animals received, for example, depended largely upon the class with which they were imaginatively associated. Deer, long protected in England for the sport of the privileged, were seen as noble beasts; so were the pampered hounds that pursued them. But "mastiffs and mongrels were lecherous, incestuous, filthy and truculent. . . . Dogs differed in status because their owners did."[11] Contempt for the lower classes implied contempt for the animals they tended. This resulted in indifference to the way most such domestic animals were treated. The care of the cart-horse was not governed by the same ethic as the care of the racehorse. Abuse of the lower classes also tempted the recipients to pass abuse down the chain of life.

Without fear of criticism the poor could beat the stock with whom they worked.

As social styles changed, these changes were reflected in the way nature was treated.

> So close was the relationship of trees to human society that their treatment, like that of horses or children, fluctuated according to changing educational fashion. In the sixteenth and early seventeenth centuries infants were swaddled; and it was widely held that most children would need to be beaten and repressed. Timber trees, correspondingly, were to be pollarded (i.e. beheaded), lopped or shredded (by cutting off the side branches). Hedges had to be regularly laid and trimmed . . .
>
> In the eighteenth century, when educational theories became less repressive, the cultivation of trees moved from regimentation to spontaneity. There was a reaction against 'mutilating' trees or carving them into "unnatural" shapes.[12]

Some who criticized the prevailing social hierarchies also protested this class-bound treatment of nature. Many Puritans, among them John Milton, believed that humans were not essentially distinct from the rest of nature. When the Puritan civil war in England released the energies of a multitude of social reformers, a few of these, some of whom came from the ranks of the poor, included all creatures in their agenda for liberation. "God loves the creatures that creep on the ground as well as the best saints," said one, "and there is no difference between the flesh of a man and the flesh of a toad."[13] In 1641 the Puritan Massachusetts Bay colony passed the first modern law concerning animal welfare: it forbade "tyranny or cruelty towards any brute creatures which are usually kept for the use of man."[14]

Nevertheless, in the eighteenth and nineteenth centuries the developing industrial revolution deepened human alienation from other natural life. When nature was viewed less as a partner and more as a collection of commodities for exploitation, the interests of the worker became dissociated from the welfare of nature. In the late nineteenth century, the development of agricultural machinery stimulated rural depopulation, and farmers who used the new machinery found their sensory contact with living things diminished. They were encouraged to adopt the dispassionate viewpoint of the scientist, to shape nature into the uniformity required for mechanical cultivation. In the twentieth century, agriculture became "agribusiness."[15]

On the other hand, a growing middle class, physically separated from nature, began to develop new attitudes. In England this class adopted from the gentry the practice of keeping pets. The splendidly landscaped estates of the aristocracy, which revitalized the English rural environment in the 1700s, were joined in the following century by tended gardens around the homes of the middle class and, where possible, around workers' cottages as well. Urban culture began to adopt nature for recreation. As animals became marginal to the processes of production, public pressure grew for standards of animal welfare. Thomas notes that, characteristically, "the concern for animal welfare was part of a much wider movement which involved the spread of humane feelings toward previously despised human beings, like the criminal, the insane or the enslaved."[16]

In the nineteenth century wild scenery was rediscovered. Pastoral landscapes, dotted with sheep and haystacks, fell from artistic favor. So much land was now under cultivation that these seemed boring, and aesthetic taste turned to wild vistas of untamed lands. John Wesley Powell, army engineer and self-trained geologist, was the first to penetrate the Grand Canyon by boat on the treacherous Colorado River. In 1869 he found communion with the rocks, deep within the gorge, to be a spiritual experience.

> Clouds are playing in the cañon to-day. Sometimes they roll down in great masses, filling the gorge with gloom; sometimes they hang above, from wall to wall, and cover the cañon with a roof of impending storm; and we can peer long distances up and down this cañon corridor, with its cloud roof overhead, its walls of black granite, and its river bright with the sheen of broken waters. Then, a gust of

wind sweeps down a side gulch, and, making a rift in the clouds, reveals the blue heavens, and a stream of sunlight pours in. Then, the clouds drift away into the distance, and hang around crags, and peaks, and pinnacles, and towers, and walls, and cover them with a mantle, that lifts from time to time, and sets them all in sharp relief. Then, baby clouds creep out of side cañons, glide around points, and creep back again, into more distant gorges. . . . The clouds are children of the heavens, and when they play among the rocks, they lift them to the region above.[17]

In both England and America, vacationers from the cities sought out the wild areas. They supported the establishment of vast public parks where nature might be protected. Wilderness itself was becoming a pet of human culture.

* * *

Modern attitudes toward nature have been shaped, in summary, by four particular factors which condition our direct experience of other life and the natural environment. *Scientific methodology*, which emphasizes dispassionate observation and detached manipulation, has repressed our intuitive empathy and weakened our emotional sensitivity to other forms of life. We also burden nature with *disordered projection*. When we are uncomfortable with sensations, desires, feelings, and needs that are part of our biological nature, we project onto animals what we fear and then treat animals in ways that express our self-rejection. Social *class structures* that encourage some persons to subordinate others, train us in attitudes of dominion and patterns of abuse which we then employ with nature. *Economic need* and economic opportunity distort society's attitude toward nature. This is particularly true at the extremes: the desperately poor are driven to consume their environment without reflection, while those who have gained power and wealth through exploitation of other people care just as little for their impact upon the natural world. Nature is affected by the quality of life within the human community.

7. London, 1842

In 1842 Charles Darwin fled the turmoil of London for a peaceful village in Kent. Eight years before, he had returned from his historic voyage to the Galápagos Islands where he first glimpsed evidence of biological evolution. Although he had tried to develop his theory while engaging with the stimulating society of scientists in this city, he could not stand the pace, the competitive pressure. Months before he left London he wrote to a friend,

> It has been a bitter mortification for me to digest the conclusion that the "race is for the strong," and that I shall probably do little more but be content to admire the strides others make in science.[1]

That same year Friedrich Engels, who would become Karl Marx's intellectual collaborator, arrived in London. He had come from Germany to study "the great towns" of the English industrial revolution. London was not a manufacturing center, but it was the center of finance and the intellectual and cultural heart of Britain, where the ethos of modern industrialism took shape. This London is remembered through the writings of Charles Dickens: choked with persons from every part of England fighting for a place in a world not yet shaped; teeming with men, women, and children who often lived in incredible poverty; overflowing with vitality and corruption; noisy with a chaos of carts, carriages, and animals; dimmed by thick, poisonous smog. Engels described it as "a war of all against all":

> We know well enough that this isolation of the individual—the narrow-minded egotism—is everywhere the

fundamental principle of modern society. But nowhere is this selfish egotism so blatantly evident as in the frantic bustle of the great city. The disintegration of society into individuals, each guided by his private principles and each pursuing his own aims, has been pushed to its furthest limits in London. Here indeed human society has been split into its component atoms.[2]

While this dismal London landscape depressed Darwin, it would stimulate Engels and Marx, and through them it has left its imprint on modern understanding of human society. Even our image of biological nature has been influenced by this London scene.

Darwin's perspective was shaped by other landscapes as well. In his brilliant study of the history of ecological thought, Donald Worster suggested that the young Darwin had a romantic fascination with violence. During the voyage around the world, which would take him to the Galápagos, he noticed over and again "the universal signs of violence."[3] On the Argentine pampas, for example, Darwin saw that an entire native ecosystem had been destroyed by the invasion of European settlers with their plants, insects, and cattle. "The countless herds of horses, cattle, and sheep not only have altered the whole aspect of the vegetation, but they have almost banished the guanaco, deer, and ostrich."[4]

By contrast, winds and tides had brought relatively few species to the young, volcanic Galápagos Islands. These species had evolved in unique ways to fill the niches of an ecological system. The novelty of the scene stimulated Darwin's curiosity, and the relative simplicity of the ecosystem helped him to grasp how it had developed. But the Galápagos, also, were a depressing place to persons with a northern sensibility. Herman Melville would visit them and remain haunted by their ugliness. "In no world but a fallen one could such lands exist. . . . I can hardly resist the feeling that . . . I have indeed slept upon evilly enchanted ground."[5] The stark Galápagos landscape would permeate Darwin's evolutionary images.

In 1838, while living in what he called "dirty, odious

London," Darwin read the Reverend Thomas Malthus' *Essay on Population*, written forty years before. Distraught by the famines and the human dislocation brought on by industrialization, Malthus hypothesized that food resources can increase only in arithmetic progression (2-3-4-5), whereas population grows at a geometric rate (2-4-8-16). Population must eventually overtake food supply, he concluded, and bring mass starvation. Darwin immediately applied Malthus' idea to the competition within species—to plants which produced an abundance of seed, and to animals which produced large litters. Only a few of the many potential offspring would survive; the most adaptive would be among these.

> It at once struck me that under these circumstances favourable variations would tend to be preserved and unfavourable ones to be destroyed. The result of this would be the formation of new species.[6]

There is profound irony in the resulting progression of thought. When Darwin published *On the Origin of the Species* in 1859, he assumed that all evolving biological characteristics bend to accommodate environmental circumstances—except this Malthusian drive to overpopulate. Population pressure was the engine for biological adaptation. But reproductive patterns—the engine itself—did not evolve or adapt. Darwin did not imagine that species might modify their reproductive behavior to accommodate themselves to their environment. Malthus' shaky hypothesis concerning human reproduction would not likely have survived into the late nineteenth century as an influence on social policy were it not that, thanks to Darwin, biological science now seemed to confirm that this principle applied to all species. Struggle and competition became the respectable, scientific characterization for all existence—biological, economic, or political.

Once he read Malthus, Darwin saw struggle everywhere: all of nature was like London. He wrote, "It is difficult to believe in the dreadful but quiet war of organic beings going on [in] the peaceful woods & smiling fields."[7] When Darwin's theory was accepted as fundamental biological truth, capitalists took it as confirmation that their competitive struggle was anchored in life's verities. Personal charity, labor unions, or social welfare programs would simply clog the process of social evolution and delay the task of exploiting and then discarding the unfit. When nature also was seen to be as ruthlessly competitive as London was, this lent credibility to the arguments of those who wished to enforce unbridled competition throughout human society.

Such an image of struggle helped to justify the new applications of technology to agriculture, forestry, fishing, and mining. If, in the contest among species, the most fit survive, then there seemed little reason to fear the worldwide spread of selected life forms supported by human ingenuity. These changes were seen to stand in the line of evolutionary progress. As industrial techniques spread to agriculture, the historic sense of "cultivation"—cooperating with sun and soil to produce crops—was replaced by images of engineering and conflict. All inputs were managed; soil, once alive with nutrients, was depleted, a sterile receptacle for hybrid seed, irrigation water, and artificial fertilizer; while life—in the form of weeds, insects, molds, and bacteria—was fought off with poison chemicals. Simple, temporary systems created by human engineering were thought to be adequate substitutes for, or indeed improvements upon, living ecosystems. Humanity, eager to compete and conquer, declared war on nature itself.

* * *

Darwin's evolutionary insights formed the foundation of modern biology and ecological science. However, the gloom that infused these insights is more a product of social reflection than biological investigation.[8]

Donald Worster pointed out that the evolution of reproduction rates, like that of other physiological characteristics, must reflect interplay with environmental characteristics: "An organism that persistently overran its food supply would not long survive; therefore the effect of natural selection on fertility would be to harmonize this characteristic with its setting, not put the two at odds." The Malthusian ratios are false, except under circumstances of profound environmental or social disturbance. More typical circumstances were reflected in young Jonathan Edwards' observation of how birthrate balanced predation and natural forces to perpetuate a relatively stable population of spiders. If Darwin's thinking on reproduction had been consistent with the rest of his theory, "it . . . would have drastically diminished the emphasis on violence and conflict in nature."9

In Darwin's theory, the competition between species was competition for "places," which ecologists have come to call "niches." These are particular positions in the environment or on the food chain. In the Galápagos, grass-eating turtles occupied several niches which in other ecosystems are occupied by cattle. Aldo Leopold noticed that when humans wish to be predators and hunt deer, they often want to get rid of the wolves and mountain lions. Humans seized a niche from the deer's natural predators.

Yet Darwin also recognized that this competition often produces results other than such displacement. Species may evolve to establish entirely new niches for themselves, thus enriching the ecosystem with new complexity. As species diverge in new directions, more forms of life are supported in the same area. Darwin noted that the enormous variety of species in the world is the consequence of this evolutionary divergence where species "opened *fresh* means of adding to their complexity. . . . Without enormous complexity, it is impossible to cover *whole* surface of world with life."10 This principle of *divergence* illustrates the creative and cooperative dimensions in evolution. Darwin recognized an important truth but did not give it sufficient emphasis. He underplayed divergence because it did not fit his need to project competition and struggle onto nature.

It is ironic that Darwin, weary of the struggle for recognition in London, himself diverged. He found his niche in a country house in Kent where he pursued his studies in increasing solitude for forty years. "I think I was never in a more perfectly quiet country . . . We are absolutely at the extreme verge of the world . . . with nothing to suggest the neighborhood of London."[11] He needed peace for his creativity. Had he not left London, he might never have produced *On the Origin of the Species* and *The Descent of Man*. Yet even sustained by the peaceful countryside, he remained prisoner to his fears of competition and his projections of violence .

* * *

Karl Marx was quick to criticize Darwin. He charged that Darwin justified English social exploitation by projecting free competition onto the animal kingdom, and saw among the beasts and plants his own English society, "with its division of labour, competition, opening up of new markets, 'inventions' and the Malthusian 'struggle for existence.' "[12] Marx did not want biology mobilized to defend capitalism, but he did not oppose human domination of nature. The oppression which concerned Marx was that of the human working class, not of lands or livestock. Indeed, Marx heralded the "great civilising influence of capital" because it had finally ended the "deification of nature."[13] He saw in the new human capabilities to exploit nature a material ground for the historical dialectic that would eventually lead to prosperity for a working class when it took control of the means of production.

Friedrich Engels was personally sensitive to feelings of domesticated animals.[14] However, along with Fourier, Saint-Simon and other nineteenth-century socialists, he wanted a clear intellectual separation of humanity from the animal kingdom and complete human control over inferior species. The exploitation of one class by another was to be replaced by expanded human exploitation of nature, made possible by new technologies and industrial techniques.[15]

Neither scientists, capitalists, nor socialists felt alarm at the growing human abuse of natural systems. In the nineteenth century, London was triumphant. The struggles of urban, industrial humanity filled the intellectual landscape of those who were shaping the future. Scientists, capitalists, and revolutionaries alike were fascinated by the heady possibilities of exploitation.

Regard for nature, in the sense of a moral concern for the welfare of natural life, was pushed to the margins of Western culture until nearly the end of the nineteenth century. Contemptuously, it was relegated to "aesthetes" and "romantics." In America, Henry David Thoreau and John Muir were such deviant voices. Gradually they gained the attention of portions of the middle class who were finding the rewards of urban life inadequate, who sought rural retreats and recreation in natural environments.

John Muir was an inventive genius who knew the excitement of industrial enterprise. As a boy on a homestead farm in Wisconsin, however, he felt the pain of disappearing wilderness, and eventually the call of the wild proved a stronger attraction than industry. Muir found his mission in California's Yosemite. There he read the rocks and discovered the impact of glaciation; he listened to nature and discovered moral value in natural life. Muir became a prophet, a "John Baptist" calling urban Americans to experience nature and to protect the wild before it was destroyed. The first book of this series describes Muir's sensuous capacity to engage with life and beauty. To a remarkable degree his whole personality—muscles, senses, emotions, intellect—was tuned to the wilderness.

I believe that when we develop such capacities as Muir did, we have an opportunity to transcend the fearful projections that alienate humans from nature. If we imagine that the struggle for survival pits us against nature, both human civilization and nature will lose. The consequences of such competition can be catastrophic. In our effort to know nature, we need our full physical, sensual, intellectual, and moral capacities. We need healing. I turn now to ideas which may help Christians overcome our fears of these very capacities.

8. *Affections*

Jonathan Edwards considered "affections" to be at the heart of human experience and human expression. Edwards did not conceive of either "will" or "reason" as distinct organs of the soul but—rejecting the traditional *faculty psychology* which has infused Western thinking—he subsumed both will and reason into the affections, which he portrayed as an integrated expression of the whole human personality.

John Locke's stress on the role of sensations in forming the human personality had liberated Edwards' thinking, but his analysis carried him further than Locke. He agreed with Locke that mental activity springs from sensory contact with the outer world: affections, like sensations, relate us to an object. Yet affections embrace the psychic activity of emotion in addition to the passivity of sensation. On the other hand, while affections include emotion, they are not merely feelings; they are feelings *about* something, feelings linked to the outer world, which stimulates our sensations. "Affections," as Edwards used the term, embraced the relation of subject with object more completely than Locke's "sensations"—and, for that matter, more adequately than the "feelings" and "emotions" considered by modern psychotherapists. I find Edwards' archaic term distinctly useful.

Modern "humanistic" psychologies, which build upon the insights of Sigmund Freud, use the image of a "whole," integrated personality to express their ideal of human health. They emphasize emotional contact, which the Greeks called Eros. "Eros was nothing but the self come vividly to life, not the self as distinguished from society, not

the ego as distinguished from the id, but the self as the
ongoing creative interplay of the organism and its total
environment, including society."[1] This characterization of
Paul Goodman's "Gestalt" psychology is a striking equivalent, in contemporary language, to Edwards' thought about
affections.

Christians need to update our psychological assumptions in order to continue relevant moral reflection. We
often utilize an implicit but unexamined faculty psychology, a
theory developed in ancient Greece and presumed throughout
the Roman, medieval, and early modern eras. Medieval and
Reformation theologians used this psychology. We inherit
its biases through our theological traditions, even though
we no longer deliberately employ this theory to understand
human personality.

Faculty psychology implied a hierarchy of internal,
mental control. The reason supervises the will, and the will
governs emotions; in a disordered, sinful personality, emotions cloud the reason and break the will. Moral teachings
and religious practices built upon this psychology tend to be
repressive. The implicit goal is self-control, the virtue cultivated by the ancient Stoics, rather than self-expression,
though expressive virtue may be more compatible with the
biblical injunctions "to *act* justly, to *love* tenderly and to *walk*
humbly with your God" (Micah 6:8, JB, emphasis added). The
practical result of this repressive moral strategy is not likely to
be a "whole" or "integrated" personality. It is more likely that a
split consciousness will result, with one part of the mind anxiously watching another. Images of mental hierarchy and control do not lead toward the moral beauty of expressive action;
instead they encourage timidity, guilt, and anxiety.

Most modern Christians are unaware of the influence
of this hidden theory. It is an antiquated, unexamined
residue from the past, deriving not from biblical thought but
from intervening traditions. Edwards' replacement for this
psychology was so far ahead of his time that it was lost in the
evolution of Christian understanding. But Edwards' insights

are overdue in Christian churches today. Although his language is sometimes antique, Edwards can help bring Christian psychological reflection into the arena of modern understanding.

Faculty psychology divided the human mind or soul into reason, the will, and affections. These mental faculties were analogous to sense organs; like the eye, ear, and nose, they supported the same mind but had separate responsibilities. Edwards used these terms also, but he maintained that the affections are so important as to embrace the others. Without active affections, neither the reason nor the will could operate.

> Such is man's nature, that he is very inactive, any otherwise than he is influenced by some affection . . . We see the world of mankind to be exceedingly busy and active; and the affections of men are the springs of the motion; take away all love and hatred, all hope and fear, all anger, zeal and affectionate desire, and the world would be, in a great measure, motionless and dead.[2]

He went on systematically to subordinate both human reasoning and human volition to the affectionate capacity.

Edwards won the admiration of eighteenth-century Calvinists for his definitive refutation of "free will." The debate concerning freedom of the will, which had continued throughout the Christian era, was rooted in faculty psychology's identification of the will as a discrete organ within the human soul. The concept of free will appealed to the subjective human experience of feeling self-directed, and it was supported by those Christian traditions which emphasized the need for human decision in achieving a saving relationship with God. In opposition to the idea of free will were those who believed that the will, like every other natural phenomenon, must depend upon causes, and also the Christian traditions emphasizing the inability of humans to find salvation without the gracious intervention of God.

Edwards resolved the claim of free will by folding the will into the affections. Saint Thomas Aquinas, in affirming free will, had concluded that the will *chooses* the greatest good perceived. However, Edwards argued that the will *exists* only because of a perception of good which brings the will to life. He set forth his famous definition of the will: "The will always is as the greatest apparent good is."[3] The crux of the definition lies in the "is as":

> I have rather chosen to express myself thus, that the will always *is* as the greatest apparent good, or as what appears most agreeable, is, than to say that the will is *determined* by the greatest apparent good, or by what seems most agreeable; because an appearing most agreeable or pleasing to the mind, and the mind's preferring and choosing, seem hardly to be properly and perfectly distinct.[4]

Thus the capacity to will springs from relationship, from a desire met by an object of that desire. Will springs from affection.

> The will, and the affections of the soul, are not two faculties; the affections are not essentially distinct from the will, nor do they differ from the mere actings of the will and inclination of the soul, but only in the liveliness and sensibleness of exercise. . . . The will never is in any exercise any further than it is affected; it is not moved out of a state of perfect indifference, any otherwise than as it is affected one way or other, and acts nothing any further.[5]

By blending the will with the affections and collapsing the traditional distinction drawn from faculty psychology, Edwards was laying a foundation for an understanding of something more significant: freedom of the person. The freedom that we experience—that we seek to enhance—is not the freedom of some portion of our psyche to operate independently of other portions. It is our freedom to act in the world, with an integrity which joins our outward affections and our deepest desires.

Contemporary psychology and psychotherapy, having abandoned faculty psychology, do not address the question of "free will" as such. But humanist psychologies deal with the concern that persons bring their "true" desires to consciousness—desires which may have been repressed under layers of anxiety, guilt, or fear; desires which may have been distorted into pallid, unsatisfying substitutes or angry opposites of their original thrust. Psychotherapy has replaced speculation about free will with concern to help persons become aware of their desires through creative engagement with life.

Edwards also subordinated reason to the affections, but he died leaving some of his best thoughts on this relationship still unpublished. His thoughts about reason remain in advance of prevailing modern attitudes. In some respects Edwards anticipated the radical or Marxist critique of "objective" reasoning. Western culture has come to exalt "detached," "scientific" reasoning, failing to notice how it is conditioned by cultural prejudice, the social position of the thinker, and even the funding source for the research. Edwards' description of our reasoning power suggests some limitations of this modern perspective.

Edwards held that the ability to reason is enhanced by affectionate engagement with the material under consideration. He sharply distinguished "sensible knowledge" from "mere speculative knowledge." Sensible knowledge, which includes sensory awareness and emotional engagement, is more useful, because it can actually influence human behavior. An experience of beauty "not only removes the hindrances of reason, but positively helps reason" to fulfill its function, Edwards explained. "It makes even the speculative notions the more lively. It engages the attention of the mind." [6]

In fact, common experience confirms that our minds usually work best when we care deeply about something. We are then motivated to reach for insights or to solve problems. When we are engaged we will also do our best academic work and are more likely to make a contribution to knowledge. Scientific culture assumes that objectivity is assisted by emotional detachment. In truth, however, emotional detachment may lead to weak reasoning, dull presentation, and conclusions that conform to the views of one's peers.

The true route to objectivity is more complex. "Objectivity" has little to do with being detached or dispassionate.

It signifies integrity in relation to one's culture, including respect for the procedures of investigation and standards of argument that our society values. We are objective when our commitment to a particular insight or discovery is balanced by regard for those to whom we communicate: we speak in terms they can understand; we disclose the evidence fully; and we do not manipulate others to our point of view. Truth is most likely to emerge in an open dialogue among involved thinkers. Truth requires a healthy social ecology within which dedicated, engaged persons from diverse backgrounds can draw together to explore a matter of common concern.

* * *

In the next chapter I will draw from the thought of Wilhelm Reich (1897-1957), an innovative protégé of Sigmund Freud, to complement Edwards' integrated psychological understanding of human expressiveness. Since Reich is not well known, I will introduce him here. He pioneered "holistic" psychotherapy by paying attention to the physical component of emotional responses. He documented that emotional inhibition is often anchored in specific muscular tensions, and he emphasized the contribution of unimpaired breathing to emotional health. Reich's principal therapeutic goal was to free sexual expression by releasing those blocks that hold desires below the level of awareness and interfere, therefore, with the successful discharge of sexual energy. He believed that satisfying sexual expression with an appropriate partner could heal neuroses—inner conflicts that cause us pain and that inspire us to exploit others or tempt us to submit to exploitation.

Historic Christian reticence about affectionate engagement with nature is closely associated with Christian anxiety about sexuality. These feelings have biblical roots which I will consider in detail in the third book of this series. Briefly, ancient Hebrew sensibilities were shaped by centuries of competition with the cult of Baal. Religious prostitution was a feature of that popular Canaanite cult, and farmers used

sympathetic sexual acts to encourage crop fertility. Since the
Hebrews worshiped a God who did not engage with the world
through sexual coupling, they came to believe that human
sexual expression was inappropriate to worship and irrelevant to agriculture. However, a long and bitter religious contest with the Baal cult led some Hebrews to develop a deeper
suspicion of sexuality. Centuries later, when primitive
Christianity developed in the urban centers of the Roman
empire, removed from the Promised Land and without hope
of political influence, Christians further "spiritualized" their
faith by devaluing both the natural world and the human
body. Even after the Catholic Church achieved political influence, the quest for a moral relationship with a beloved land
was not renewed within the church, and refraining from sexual expression was encouraged as a discipline to prepare oneself to leave this world for a better one.

Reich had a particular interest in sexual functioning.
Working with Sigmund Freud during the 1920s, he took
Freud's early understanding of *libido* and developed it into a
more radical theory of the importance of sexuality to human
health. Reich believed we have been trained to fear and to
repress our sexuality; this, he declared, is the basic cause of
neuroses. His cure was to help people unblock their sexual
energy and achieve orgasmic potency—not just an "orgasm"
in the popular modern sense, but a cycle of tension and spas-
modic discharge that released the flow of energy through the
entire body. Reich advanced his patients toward such potency
by helping them soften a sequence of muscular blocks that
had resulted from emotional trauma, freeing their breathing,
their feelings, and their sense of vitality.

First as a Communist in Vienna, then in Berlin as a
public opponent of Adolf Hitler's growing power, Reich was
also the most political of Freud's disciples. His analysis of
Hitler's irrational attraction proved prophetic. Reich saw
that Hitler exploited the people's deep sexual repressions,
promising them a more exciting life while also reinforcing
their fears of expression through demands for rigorous "law

and order." Hitler then bled these heightened tensions by erecting the Jew as a scapegoat toward whom popular anger could be expressed, projecting a paranoiac picture of Jews as seducers, castrators, and Shylocks.

Reich's impulsive political counterattack was well-meant but simplistic. In Berlin he organized vast public sex-education sessions in an emergency program to help the masses free their repressions and therefore develop immunity to Hitler's appeals. Although the sessions were popular, Reich's supporters became alarmed at his advocacy of sexual freedom for children and adolescents, abortion on demand, and sexual experimentation by adults. The Communist party, his original sponsor, withdrew its support. Fearful of scandal which would discredit his young movement, Sigmund Freud approved Reich's removal from his Psychoanalytic Association.

In 1939, Reich fled to the United States. Though he continued teaching and practicing psychotherapy, he concentrated on furthering his orgasm theory through biological and electrophysical research. He believed he had isolated the basic, pulsating form of energy that underlies all forms of organic life. Reich called it *orgone*, and he developed insulated compartments for stimulating and reflecting the flow of this energy. He found these "accumulators" useful in healing wounds, even in treating cancers. Since Reich associated "orgone" with "orgasm," popular imagination fantasized that the "orgone accumulator" that Reich employed was a device for sexual arousal. It was not, but again Reich's work was the subject of scandal. He grew self-protective and paranoid, while his biophysical theories attracted little attention from the scientific community.[7]

In 1954 the Food and Drug Administration moved to block the distribution of orgone accumulators, since FDA tests did not show that they had any medical effect. This might have been an occasion for the scientific scrutiny of his biophysical theories which Reich had once wished for. But the FDA's approach was hostile and patronizing, and Reich—thoroughly paranoid now—refused to appear in court or to make reasonable use of his administrative and legal opportunities. The FDA obtained a court order requiring not only the destruction of all accumulators, but the burning of all Reich's books and publications that made any mention of "orgone energy." On August 23, 1956, FDA agents came to Reich's center in Maine to supervise the burning of his books and literature. This was a low point in the history of freedom of speech in America. Reich himself was imprisoned for contempt of court, and died in federal prison on November 3, 1957.

Reich had few defenders at the end. For years following his death the ambitious in psychotherapy avoided his name. Nevertheless, Reich's theories and techniques were the fountainhead of the humanistic schools of psychotherapy that modified orthodox Freudianism. Since the mid-1960s, such therapies have become increasingly popular: encounter groups, Gestalt therapy, bioenergetics, radix therapy, and others. In the 1980s it is finally becoming acceptable to mention Reich's name and acknowledge his influence.

I was introduced to Wilhelm Reich's perspective when my wife, Anne, took training in Gestalt psychotherapy, and then when my own therapist employed some of Reich's techniques. I became acquainted with his daughter, Dr. Eva Reich, a pediatrician and psychotherapist who combines loyalty to her father's insights with a deep faith in Jesus. Eva Reich, my wife Anne, and I have together conducted a workshop for Christians in ministry on faith and sexuality. I believe many Christians need to appreciate our own sexuality and express emotions more fully if we are able to rejoice in the Lord and embrace the world God made.

9. *Insensibility*

That perverse human quality Christians call "sin" includes our capacity to hurt ourselves and others. Many believers associate sin with sensuality, and the more intellectual Christians usually link it to selfishness. Jesus, by contrast, often associated sin with *insensibility*—our determined, seemingly willful inability to feel or perceive.

> If you have ears, then hear. How can I describe this generation? They are like children sitting in the market-place and shouting at each other,
> > "We piped for you and you would not dance."
> > "We wept and wailed, and you would not mourn."
> > (Matthew 11:15–17, NEB)

By his characteristic admonition "If you have ears, then hear," Jesus implied that the sensibility of his hearers would determine their capacity to receive his message. Yet when Jesus explained to his disciples why he used vivid images and parables to communicate with the crowds, he despaired that even these would arouse their sensibility. Jesus suggested that the crowd feared hearing because hearing might open them to change:

> The reason I talk to them in parables is that they look without seeing and listen without hearing or understanding. So in their case what was spoken by the prophet Isaiah is being fulfilled:
>
> > *Listen and listen, but never understand!*
> > *Look and look, but never perceive!*
> > *This people's heart has grown coarse,*
> > *their ears dulled, they have shut their eyes tight*
> > *to avoid using their eyes to see, their ears to hear,*

> *their heart to understand,*
> *changing their ways and being healed by me.*

> But blessed are your eyes because they see, your
> ears because they hear! In truth I tell you, many prophets
> and upright people longed to see what you see, and never
> saw it; to hear what you hear, and never heard it.
>
> (Matthew 13:13–17, NJB)[1]

Here Jesus described a surprisingly common human
condition: people fear sensibility even though open senses
might lead to healing.

"This is the *armor*," said Wilhelm Reich, reflecting on
this comment by Jesus.[2] Reich believed that fears of sensibility were not just in the mind. He found that neurotic fear of
feelings manifests in abnormal muscular tension, creating an
armor that blocks the flow of emotions.

Reich stressed the importance of pleasure. He believed that in Western culture the very idea of pleasure
creates anxiety, partly because of the sexual anxiety which
Christian churches have encouraged. Resistance to pleasure
is also rooted in our fear of pain: if we armor ourselves
against all feelings, we can avoid much that is painful. These
anxieties are transmitted from parents to children and
enforced by what Reich called our "six-thousand-year-old
patriarchal authoritarian culture."[3]

A child copes with anxiety by developing a "charac-
terological armoring against his inner nature and against the
social misery which surrounds him."[4] The armoring, often
visible in the chronic tension of certain muscle groups, blocks
or weakens the reception of sensations from outside oneself.
It also blocks the personality's flow, both upward to consciousness and outward in expression:

> . . . conventional upbringing makes people incapable of
> pleasure by armoring them against unpleasure. *Pleasure*
> *and joy of life are inconceivable without struggle, painful*
> *experiences, and unpleasurable self-confrontations.* . . . the
> ability to endure unpleasure and pain without becoming
> embittered and seeking refuge in rigidification goes hand in
> hand with the ability to receive happiness and to give love.[5]

It is noteworthy that although Reich's theory of repression at first appears to be tightly focused on the problems of genital sexuality, he in fact introduced a second, broader reason for the cultural encouragement of repression: a general fear of pain. We harden ourselves and we harden our children to protect them from the pain in the world.

Here, adapted from Reich's diagrams, are step-by-step illustrations showing the development of "neurotic" character structure which is so common in our society.[6] The first stage of the diagram represents the uncomplicated expression of human affection from the human personality. An example is love expressed by a child toward a parent (Figure 1).

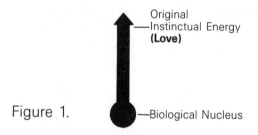

Figure 1.

If, however, the natural expression of this love meets with strong rebuke, or if the child is terrifed by the power of the parent, the child may choose to block the expression (Figure 2). The blocked expression splits into two streams of energy,

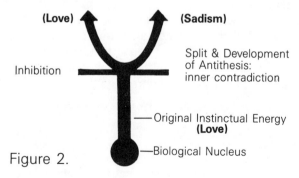

Figure 2.

the original stream and its antithesis, like a stream of water looking for an outlet. In the example one of the resulting streams is love, and the other is anger or sadism—sadism being the warped expression of love through cruelty.

This angry stream, however, must also be blocked

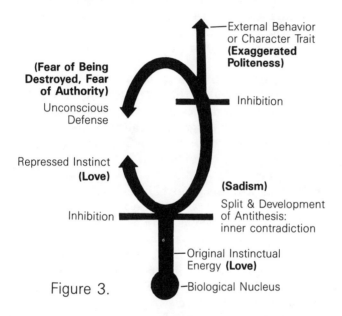

(Fear of Being Destroyed, Fear of Authority)

Unconscious Defense

—External Behavior or Character Trait **(Exaggerated Politeness)**

Inhibition

Repressed Instinct **(Love)**

(Sadism)

Inhibition

Split & Development of Antithesis: inner contradiction

—Original Instinctual Energy **(Love)**

Figure 3.

—Biological Nucleus

(Figure 3), for the child is not permitted to express it outwardly to the parent. The child may even come to push the awareness of anger out of consciousness. So at this second point of inhibition the stream of anger splits again. The child shows outwardly to the parent exaggerated politeness and calculating good behavior, the antithesis of which is fear of being destroyed and fear of authority. The child now uses these fear-laden energies to hold love in check and to keep it also below the level of awareness. Therefore, most of the child's psychic energy goes toward fighting internally and controlling emotions; only the smaller part actively engages

with the outer world. The child's capacity for affection—the
child's sensibility—is greatly diminished.

Undoubtedly, this theory simplifies complex psychological processes. However, it provided a plausible account of
how our insensibility, rooted in fear, binds our energy for living. We hide from ourselves as well as from engagement with
the world, and once we are so armored, we both receive less
from the world and we give less to the world. Much of what
we do exchange, in fact, is misleading.

Reich believed that parents inflict such damage
through repeated *moralistic prohibitions*. The term does not
apply to all moral restraints, but to those which are arbitrary
and unhealthy. A moralistic prohibition is the socially sanc-
tioned restriction of an otherwise healthy expression of emotion, enforced by the excessive use of authority by parents or
other superior persons over children or other dependent and
vulnerable persons. For example, a three-year-old who finds
pleasure playing with his penis has his hand slapped: "Don't,
that's dirty!" This parental attitude is reinforced by a culture which teaches that sex is dirty and which values sexual
innocence in children, so that childish interest in genital
pleasure is viewed with alarm. If the child persists in this
pleasure he does so secretly, learning from this hidden pleasure that he is, indeed, dirty. Reich was angered to see how
such prohibitions bind conflicts into a fear-ridden character
structure, a structure that manifests three layers in tension.

> The patriarchal, authoritarian era of human history
> has attempted to hold the asocial impulses in check by
> means of compulsive moralistic prohibitions. It is in this
> way that civilized man, if he can indeed be called civilized,
> developed a psychic structure consisting of three layers. On
> the surface, he wears an artificial mask of self-control, com-
> pulsive insincere politeness, and pseudo-sociality. This
> mask conceals the second layer, the Freudian "uncon-
> scious," in which sadism, avarice, lasciviousness, envy, per-
> versions of all kind, etc., are held in check without, however,
> being deprived of the slightest amount of energy. This sec-
> ond layer is the artificial product of a sex-negating culture
> and is usually experienced consciously as a gaping inner

emptiness and desolation. Beneath it, in the depth, natural sociality and sexuality, spontaneous joy in work, the capacity for love, exist and operate. This third and deepest layer, which represents the biological core of the human structure, is unconscious, and it is feared.[7]

Jesus condemned this multilayered, conflicted character structure in similar angry tones. He rebuked those whose outward conformity masked seething impulses.

> Alas for you, lawyers and Pharisees, hypocrites! You pay tithes of mint and dill and cumin; but you have overlooked the weightier demands of the Law, justice, mercy, and good faith. . . .
> Alas for you, lawyers and Pharisees, hypocrites! You clean the outside of cup and dish, which you have filled inside by robbery and self-indulgence! . . .
> Alas for you, lawyers and Pharisees, hypocrites! You are like tombs covered with whitewash; they look well from outside, but inside they are full of dead men's bones and all kinds of filth. (Matthew 23:23, 25, 27, NEB).

Through teaching and healing, Jesus aimed to free such self-deceived personalities. He wished men and women to be whole, to live expressively, and to discover a moral beauty that transcended traditional reason and common sense. "You shall not kill" was no longer an adequate commandment. Jesus insisted that the root of anger must be removed (Matthew 5:21–26, RSV). Nor was "Do not commit adultery" a sufficient standard; the basic desires of the heart must be pure and consistent (Matthew 5:27–28, NEB). Love limited by the conventions of society—"Love your neighbour, hate your enemy"—was also no longer adequate: "I tell you this:" Jesus directed, "Love your enemies and pray for your persecutors" (Matthew 5:43–44, NEB).

In one of his beatitudes Jesus summarized his psychological perspective: "How blest are those whose hearts are pure; they shall see God" (Matthew 5:8, NEB). Purity of heart implies that our feelings and behavior flow from our whole being, free of conflict. Our conscious emotions and our behavior toward others relate to our real character. True love and

true life are expressions of integrity. To achieve this direct-
ness we may need to be "born over again" (John 3:3–8, NEB),
opening and reforming our personality into an expressive
unity. One reason Jesus is so treasured is that he appears to
have lived the transparent purity of heart about which he
preached. In so doing he exposed the potential of the human
personality. Many have felt, in addition, that in Jesus they
have seen the beauty of God.

The Apostle Paul, in contrast, began adulthood as the
type of person Reich imagined when he wrote his angry para-
graph about the three layers of personality created in the
"patriarchal, authoritarian era of human history." Compulsive moralism led Paul to act out his loyalty to God through
vicious persecution of those who followed Jesus' more
open path.

> I am a true-born Jew . . . thoroughly trained in every
> point of our ancestral law. I have always been ardent in
> God's service. . . . And so I began to persecute this move-
> ment to the death, arresting its followers, men and women
> alike, and putting them in chains. (Acts 22:3–4, NEB)

Even after his dramatic conversion to Christianity, Paul carried with him struggles from this past. Often his deeds and
words witnessed to a new, clear vitality, but at other times he
wrestled with his own conflicts.

Paul's analysis of human nature reflected his continuing anxiety about how the forces below the surface of the
human personality might break through when not held in
check by the law. Despite outward appearances, Paul said,
people are

> filled with all manner of wickedness, evil, covetousness,
> malice. Full of envy, murder, strife, deceit, malignity, they
> are gossips, slanderers, haters of God, insolent, haughty,
> boastful, inventors of evil, disobedient to parents, foolish,
> faithless, heartless, ruthless. (Romans 1:29–31, RSV)

Paul's listing is similar to Reich's description of the second
layer of the neurotic personality.

Renewed through his dramatic conversion to faith in Jesus, Paul grew to proclaim liberation from dependence upon the law. Christians are to act freely from the whole heart, he declared. At the same time, though, Paul confessed to his own inner struggles, his continuing sense of a layered personality, to erratic behavior, and to self-condemnation. "I do not understand my own actions. For I do not do what I want, but I do the very thing I hate. . . . I see in my members another law at war with the law of my mind" (Romans 7:15, 23, RSV). Reich pointed out that this kind of inner warfare is "experienced consciously as a gaping inner emptiness and desolation." Paul, tormented by those very emotions, cried out, "Wretched man that I am! Who will deliver me from this body of death?" (Romans 7:24, RSV).

Of course, Paul could follow his agonized question with a heartfelt answer: "Thanks be to God through Jesus Christ our Lord! . . . There is therefore now no condemnation for those who are in Christ Jesus" (Romans 7:25, 8:1, RSV). Despite his moments of panic, Paul knew himself freed from the law, freed from the need for self-condemnation, open to the possibility of living a whole and expressive life. Militantly he proclaimed this precious liberty. "For freedom Christ has set us free; stand fast therefore, and do not submit again to a yoke of slavery" (Galatians 5:1, RSV).

Though he would relapse from time to time into internal conflict, though he would retreat under pressure into legalism, moralism, paternalism, and sexism, the freedom Paul won was nevertheless real in his experience. He knew he was open to the beauty of God. Whatever the imperfections of his knowledge and his prophecy, love was now able to flow. His faith was not an anxious hope, but a basic trust. He had a calm, inner assurance that the tensions he still experienced would be resolved. "I shall understand fully, even as I have been fully understood. So faith, hope, love abide, these three; but the greatest of these is love" (1 Corinthians 13:12–13, RSV).

* * *

Both life-repairing psychology and a redeeming spirituality must help a person express affections and build a life
that flows from them with integrity. As I bring my desires to
consciousness, and express my energies in living, I am challenged to build relationships—both meaningful and moral—
with people and with the requirements of society. However,
it is not appropriate for culture to induce me to block desires
below awareness. Mahatma Gandhi, the apostle of nonviolence, affirmed this insight in a parable. "What am I to
advise a man to do who wants to kill but is unable owing to
his being maimed? Before I can make him feel the virtue of
not killing, I must restore to him the arm he has lost."[8]

Troubling questions follow from my conclusion that
expressing human affections is extremely important. Can a
social institution like the Pharisaic community of old or the
Christian community of today avoid endorsing superficial
morality? Will we not inevitably encourage repression of
basic desires? How can a culture support expression?

In a world filled with pain, is it responsible to encourage the development of greater human capacity to feel?
For billions of crowded, hungry, oppressed people, is there a
potential for pleasure which justifies the risk of greater pain?
Would it not be better for religion to remain what Karl Marx
called it, an "opiate for the people"? Many opiates seem to be
desired, and the church has often been a compassionate
source of such. Perhaps it would be unwise to stimulate
human sensibility until there has been substantial improve-
ment in social justice and human welfare. Nevertheless,
those who lead struggles for justice find that numbness from .
oppression is one of the principal barriers to change. They
cry out against opiates. I believe we must encourage all people to take the risks of feeling.

As an adolescent I was tormented by one of Jesus'
teachings to which I have already alluded:

> You have heard that it was said, "You shall not com-
> mit adultery." But I say to you that every one who looks at a
> woman lustfully has already committed adultery with her
> in his heart. If your right eye causes you to sin, pluck it out

> and throw it away; it is better that you lose one of your
> members than that your whole body be thrown into hell.
> And if your right hand causes you to sin, cut it off and throw
> it away; it is better that you lose one of your members than
> that your whole body go to hell. (Matthew 5:27–30, RSV)

I suspect that many boys in a Christian environment have
been terrified by this passage. We heard it in the context of
our awakening sexual urges and new, seemingly anarchic
fantasies. The "cutting and plucking" language told us that
we should not be having sexual urges, while the reference to
looking at a woman lustfully convinced us that we were,
already, lost in sin. This misreading is a tragic misunderstanding of Jesus' intention. Matthew took a saying of Jesus
concerning adultery and joined it with sayings found elsewhere about offending bodily parts.[9] Although the sayings
have a common message, that message is clouded when they
are placed together so threateningly.

The theme of the Sermon on the Mount is purity of
heart. Outward conformity to the law is not enough; our
actions must spring from our character. The words on adultery are not intended to propound a new standard of repression, but to illustrate again this new standard of integrity. If
you lust after a married person, refraining from the sexual
act in order to conform to social pressure does not make you
holy. Jesus' critique is not here aimed at lustfulness but at
hypocrisy. His intention is to correct those who feel virtuous
because they hold their lustfulness in check in the interest of
outward conformity. The sayings about offending bodily
parts, probably spoken in another context, carry a similar
message. We should strive for integrity and consistency.
When we have found our direction, we must resist returning
to anxious inner conflict; instead we should cut short that
debate and go on with life.

The idea of "repression" reflects a modern style of
thinking rather than a biblical one. Jesus did not advocate
repression: rather, to those who could receive his word he
offered rebirth to become whole, single-minded, expressive
men and women.

Part III.

Awakening

I was born again in June of my fifteenth year, in the tiny walled garden behind my home in Washington, D.C., two days after returning from a church camp. There, after determined resistance, I surrendered to God's clear demand that I yield my life and dedicate myself to Jesus' ministry. With that surrender I felt strength, and also a joy which remained so tangible that for the remaining months of summer I marveled at myself daily. I was excited to know who I was. God's invitation to significant service gave me a fresh feeling of worth, while my assurance of God's presence gave me courage. I had a vocation, a conviction of direction for the future, which—not incidentally—shielded me from the intense but disparate ambitions that my separated parents held for their one common child.

This "conversion" set me in the mainstream of American religious experience. Even though my liberal Presbyterian Church did not require this style of conversion, the experience was recognized and supported, particularly among those who ministered to youth. Fundamentalist, evangelical Protestants treasure this kind of conversion, and in my excitement I drew closer to such conservative Christians during my college years. But their anxious assurance of the right answer to every question was not plausible to me; it conflicted with my curiosity.

Thirsty for understanding, I looked in history and met the Great Awakening, a remarkable enthusiasm which spread through England and her American colonies during the 1730s and 1740s. Two religious geniuses, different from each other, emerged from the Great Awakening: John Wesley, the pre-eminent religious organizer, in England; and Jonathan Edwards, the philosopher of

Christian experience, in New England. Other leaders of the revival, more commonplace thinkers, were nevertheless remarkable for their vitality and enthusiasm—the Great Awakening was a work of spirit. Edwards himself, as we shall see, could say and do foolish things in the excitement of revival, but he never ceased pondering what happened, and why.

The emotional experience of conversion, supported by group enthusiasm, remains the most characteristic form of American Christian piety. This "evangelical" tradition encourages emotional expression which must, indeed, be part of a healthy religious life. Yet it also encourages the deflection of emotional energy away from the common relationships of daily life, including human interaction with the natural world. The conversion tradition supports personal efforts to integrate convictions with feelings; bodily awareness, however, is often left out of such self-understanding. Christians may remain alienated from, and suspicious of, some of their most urgent and tangible sensations. The Great Awakening initiated these patterns which have persisted in American religious culture. Remarkably, Edwards took the lead both in fanning the flames of revival and also in evaluating the consequences. His leadership, his theological reflection, and particularly his changing personal experience—along with changes in his wife, his church, and his community—reveal the great strengths and troubling limitations of this religious phenomenon. I emerge from evaluating this seminal American event with new insights about how we may experience human vitality, love for the Lord, and communion with the natural world.

10. *The Rhetoric of Revival*

In the 1740s, the Great Awakening swept through the American colonies, a vast outpouring of religious fervor beyond the control of established churches and leading churchmen. Active leaders like Jonathan Edwards stimulated the fervor but could not limit its effects. Colonial Christianity consisted primarily of territorial outposts of English denominations, each hoping to maintain its version of true faith within its sphere of influence. This lingering theocratic desire to protect religious conformity within a church's territory of jurisdiction was now undermined by a spirit blowing through the churches themselves.

The Great Awakening brought American Christianity to its distinctive form: diverse, competitive, emotional, flexible, innovative, popular, and uncontrolled. It released energies which, in civic life, would contribute to the ferment for political independence. Following the American Revolution, separation of church and state would be the appropriate constitutional response to the energetic diversity then apparent in American Christianity. The government would not try to rationalize these disparate, innovative religious energies. It would neither support churches nor inhibit religion. The churches were on their own.

Puritans had come to New England a century before the Great Awakening to establish a holy commonwealth governed by the pious—"a city set on a hill" which would represent true faith to England and Europe. When Edwards helped precipitate the awakening, he was hoping for

a revival of that ancient vigor. He was not looking to create
something new.

New England Puritans professed "experimental
piety." That is, they were convinced that when God reached a
person with saving love, the believer would experience a
change of heart and would, in most instances, be able to give
a description of this experience which other believers could
recognize as genuine. The first New England generation had
based church membership—and with it the right to vote and
participate in civic affairs—upon the petitioner's ability to
give the congregation a satisfactory account of such experience. When fervor declined in subsequent generations
Solomon Stoddard, Edwards' grandfather and predecessor in
the pulpit of Northampton, Massachusetts, proposed a compromise to allow children of professed believers to receive
communion in the hope that it would lead them to conversion. However, Puritans continued to pray for an experience
of faith which moved the heart and convinced the mind that
God was indeed extending grace toward an undeserving sinner.

The moment of conversion might be purely individual, but often such conversions occurred during periods of
awakening in a congregation or a village. The shock of a natural disaster, perhaps the affecting example of one person's
conversion, might stimulate in others feelings of repentance
and the experience of faith. Particularly among adolescents,
religious experiences might spread from one person to another. Such local seasons of awakening, affecting a handful in a
community, were common in New England. Ministers and
faithful church members prayed for such times and awaited
God's mercy.

The Great Awakening differed from these periods
both in the intensity of experiences and in the fact that, after
several local awakenings in the 1730s, the fervor spread like
wildfire from community to community. By the early 1740s
every city and most villages in the American colonies had
been touched by its power.

In America, the first local revival to exhibit the Great

Awakening's intensity occurred in 1734 in Northampton, under the preaching of Jonathan Edwards. The fervor spread quickly to neighboring villages. Edwards' detailed account of this "Surprising Work of God" was read eagerly in the American colonies and in England as well.[1] In England the preaching of John Wesley and George Whitefield, who would later be called "Methodists," had been creating similar excitement. These movements fused in 1740 when George Whitefield toured New England, New York, and Philadelphia. His amazing voice could reach five thousand people in an open field. The wildfire was ignited.

As awakening spread, some found its emotionalism offensive. Established ministers felt threatened when wandering preachers appeared and gathered large, unsupervised crowds. Some of these evangelists were no more than rabble-rousers, enjoying their power to stir emotions and create dissension; but pastors who refused to allow itinerant preachers into their pulpits might be accused of being "cold," "hardened," or "lost in their sins."

In the Middle Atlantic states these tensions split the Presbyterian Church into "New Light" and "Old Light" factions. Calvinists led this awakening in both New England and the Middle Atlantic states, but such new wine was hard to contain in old bottles. The masses who were touched by awakening experienced new feelings of worth, salted with rebellion against established churches and institutions. Preachers of denominations new to the American scene— Methodists and Baptists—harnessed the revivalist pattern most effectively, leading the spread of Christianity on the developing western frontier.

* * *

It is no accident that the American awakening began in Northampton in 1734, for that was the year Jonathan Edwards began to apply in his preaching the psychology he developed from John Locke. He began an experiment in rhetoric which, like the fabled surprise of the chemist, blew the roof off the laboratory.

Just as Puritans had stripped their churches of pictures and ornamentation, so they had rejected the flowery, poetic rhetoric of the Elizabethan era in favor of plain speaking. God's truth did not require man's embellishment. Preaching was clear, explicit, long-winded, and unbelievably dull. Edwards spoke within this tradition, but he had fresh insight about how language works. Early in 1734 he published a short sermon titled "A Divine and Supernatural Light, Immediately Imparted to the Soul by the Spirit of God." Here he applied his psychological insight to the question of how faith is formed. He explained that the mind is convinced of truth not by argument, but by experience. The function of preaching, therefore, is not to persuade, but to provide experience of the truths of the Gospel; or, rather, to place in the hearer's mind specific images which God's spirit may bring to life. According to Edwards' sermon, "He that is spiritually enlightened truly apprehends and sees" the beauty of God. "He does not merely rationally believe that God is glorious, but he has a sense of the gloriousness of God in his heart."[2]

Edwards' preaching style was sober and methodical. He did not display his emotions. Townspeople recalled that "Mr. Edwards in preaching used no gestures, but looked straight forward. . . . He looked on the bell rope until he looked it off."[3] Edwards' experiment in rhetoric was to portray biblical events and images with such precision that they became to his hearers as vivid and compelling as the experiences of daily life. He was convinced that Christian doctrines could not be saving until they were truly experienced through human senses. "Faith" he said, "is a *sensibleness* of what is real in the work of redemption."[4]

Most of Edwards' sermons dramatized God's redeeming love. His most notorious sermon, "Sinners in the Hands of an Angry God," is also a product of this rhetorical experiment, and it illustrates his technique most vividly. Edwards did not argue with his hearers about the threat of damnation, but gave them a convincing experience of the fires of hell.

The tone of the following passage was sustained, unremittingly, for an hour:

> So . . . thus it is that natural men are held in the hand of God, over the pit of hell; they have deserved the fiery pit, and are already sentenced to it; and God is dreadfully provoked, his anger is as great towards them as to those that are actually suffering the executions of the fierceness of his wrath in hell, and they have done nothing in the least to appease or abate that anger, neither is God in the least bound by any promise to hold them up one moment; the devil is waiting for them, hell is gaping for them, the flames gather and flash about them, and would fain lay hold on them, and swallow them up . . .
>
> The use of this awful subject may be for awakening unconverted persons in this congregation. This that you have heard is the case of every one of you that are out of Christ. That world of misery, that lake of burning brimstone, is extended abroad under you.

To climax his assault on his hearers' sensibility, Edwards recalled the spiders he had studied so meticulously as a child. All his affection for these creatures, however, was excised from this illustration which has chilled generations.

> You probably are not sensible of this. . . . The God that holds you over the pit of hell, much as one holds a spider, or some loathsome insect over the fire, abhors you, and is dreadfully provoked. . . .
>
> O sinner! Consider the fearful danger you are in: it is a great furnace of wrath, a wide and bottomless pit, full of the fire of wrath, that you are held over in the hand of that God, whose wrath is provoked and incensed as much against you, as against many of the damned in hell. You hang by a slender thread, with the flames of divine wrath flashing about it, and ready every moment to singe it, and burn it asunder; and you have no interest in any Mediator, and nothing to lay hold of to save yourself, nothing to keep off the flames of wrath, nothing of your own, nothing that you ever have done, nothing that you can do, to induce God to spare you one moment.[5]

An observer reported that "the assembly appeared deeply impressed and bowed down with an awful conviction of their sin and danger. There was such a breathing of distress and weeping, that the preacher was obliged to speak to the people and desire silence, that he might be heard."[6]

New England's leading critic of such emotionalism in the awakening, Charles Chauncy of Boston, charged that "passions have, generally, in these times, been apply'd to, as though the main thing in religion was to throw them into disturbance." He argued that "an enlightened mind, and not raised affections, ought always to be the guide of those who call themselves men," even in "the affairs of religion. . . . Reasonable beings are not to be guided by passion or affection," even when the object of those feelings is "God and the things of another world."[7] In response, Edwards maintained that it is "a reasonable thing to endeavor to fright persons away from hell, that stand upon the brink of it, and are just ready to fall into it, and are senseless of their danger," just as " 'tis a reasonable thing to fright a person out of an house on fire."[8]

Edwards had grasped powerful truth, but he did not understand all the components of his explosive insight. He knew the importance of experience: senses alert and emotions alive. If senses were dulled and feelings were blocked, one could lose meaningful contact with this world, and thus the experience of God might also be out of reach. However, Edwards did not appreciate the particular risk of utilizing vivid religious symbols as tools to open human sensory and emotional capacities. Religious symbols properly contribute meaning and emotional depth to the full range of human experience. However, this happens when they are grasped—not when they are imposed. And while many in Edwards' congregation were able either to grasp or reject the vivid suggestions of their preacher, some were simply overwhelmed by the images and became lost amid their power.

When a repressed person is taken captive by images presented in a religious setting, he or she may feel that the religious experience is uniquely real and may displace earlier, blocked desires onto religious images. It is satisfying to vent such feelings, but displacement neither truly expresses nor illumines them.[9] It further tangles emotions. Religious experience may indeed be so engaging that other relationships pale by comparison; a person caught up in religion may become convinced that daily life is not so real. Such a personality, however, is not integrated. Obsession with religious fervor may cause one's life to become even more difficult, so that the person remains dependent upon exotic experience in an isolated religious context.

Edwards unwittingly intruded upon the psychological integrity of some of his hearers when he so dramatized Christian symbols that religious feelings displaced expression within daily life. Today we call the deliberate, knowing use of this technique "brainwashing." Brainwashing does not have the same effect as real experience. It does not expand awareness, but rather contracts its victims, producing dependent, weak, and often angry persons. These do not resemble the loving, whole, and free persons Jesus cultivated.

Edwards knew what modern psychology is discovering again: withholding feelings does not make one rational. We now know that such withholding can lead to depression, confusion, and apathy. Edwards, however, lacked an important modern insight: if a person has blocked the flow of emotional energy toward its intended object, some of this energy may emerge as positive or negative feeling toward substitute attachments. Religious symbols, dramatically presented, can become substitute objects for human loves and fears. Rather than liberating the flow of real feelings, such religious experience perpetuates the displacement of feelings from appropriate objects. To build a whole person, religious experience must involve genuine experience of God and moral beauty. A religious experience dominated by displaced emotions cannot bring a person to renewed life.

This remains a problem in Christian proclamation. Although we are blessed with rich biblical and religious images fashioned, I believe, through real human struggle to be faithful to the Lord in this world, Christians may be tempted to use these images as substitutes for personal awareness and engagement with daily life. We may dramatize the images of our heritage until they become so real that the world of living persons and present events recedes from view. Jesus, whom the church has seen as God's saving entry into human history, can thus become a means for us to escape from life.

* * *

However, the Great Awakening was neither dominated by fear nor characterized by escape from life. Most of those caught up in the awakening joyfully discovered love and assurance, and thus lived more expressively in their daily lives. This provided the energy for the movement that spread so rapidly through colonial society. Edwards' accounts capture some of the wonder of this release. Describing persons who felt anew God's love and mercy, Edwards wrote, "Their joyful surprise has caused their hearts as it were to leap, so that they have been ready to break forth into laughter, tears often at the same time issuing like a flood and intermingling a loud weeping; and sometimes they han't been able to forbear crying out with a loud voice, expressing their great admiration." He noted that while members of his congregation were already excellent singers, using four-part harmony on some hymns, "now they were evidently wont to sing with unusual elevation of heart and voice, which made the duty pleasant indeed." Awakened persons also experienced heightened sense perception.

> The light and comfort which some of them enjoy, gives a new relish to their common blessings, and causes all things about 'em to appear as it were beautiful, sweet and pleasant to them: all things abroad, the sun, moon and stars, the clouds and sky, the heavens and earth, appear as it were with a cast of divine glory and sweetness upon them.[10]

Certainly, some persons were stalked by anxiety, despondency, and even terror during the awakening. Edwards assured his people that such feelings were appropriate responses to their new awareness of the burden of sin and the danger of separation from God. Anxiety was just a step in the process of conversion which would lead to abiding joy. His remedy was to intensify his preaching of the Gospel, until the despairing would be grasped by God's love.

Not all the despairing could be reached, however. In June of 1735 Edwards' uncle, Joseph Hawley—a pious, respected merchant—cut his own throat. Edwards recorded, "He had, from the beginning of this extraordinary time, been exceedingly concerned about the state of his soul," and when the spirit of revival waned that year, Hawley's despair intensified. He developed acute insomnia and finally took his life. Edwards was stunned. Hawley, indeed, was not alone in such emotional vulnerability. Edwards indicates that many others were so insecure and suggestible as to be cast into confusion by this tragedy.

> After this, multitudes in this and other towns seemed to have it strongly suggested to 'em, and pressed upon 'em, to do as this person had done . . . as if somebody had spoke to 'em "Cut your own throat, now is good opportunity: *now,* NOW!" So that they were obliged to fight with all their might to resist it.[11]

Edwards' experiment in rhetoric had produced abundant fruit, but some of it was not wholesome. He still had much to learn about how human personalities respond to vivid religious images.

11. *Jonathan's Experience*

The Northampton revival that led to the Great Awakening was the turning point in Jonathan Edwards' life, for it was also the context of his personal awakening. The rest of his life issued from this ferment: his desire to preach awakening, his determination both to defend the revival and chasten its more unruly partisans, his eventual rejection at the hands of his own congregation, and his deepening insight into the nature of religious experience.

In 1736, two years after the Northampton revival, Edwards wrote an account of it which was published in London the next year. Then, in 1739, just before the full wildfire of the Great Awakening ignited, Edwards wrote an autobiographical "Personal Narrative" of his religious experience, which he held from publication during his lifetime. This narrative focused on a youthful period of Christian decision from the time he graduated at age seventeen from Yale until two years later, while he was serving his brief first pastorate in a Presbyterian church in New York City. During those years he had also kept a private diary which included a list of pious resolutions. If we compare that adolescent diary with Edwards' narrative account of the same period written following the Northampton revival, we can see a remarkable growth in his ability to recognize the sensuous character of his own religious experience.

In his mature "Personal Narrative" Edwards recalled that his childhood experience of religion began "at a time of remarkable awakening in my father's congregation." Playing at religion, he joined several companions to build an equivalent of the child's tree house: "a booth in a swamp, in a very retired spot, for a place of prayer." Young Jonathan, not content with this, also developed another secret spot in the woods, known only to himself.[1]

Jonathan was an only son with ten sisters in a busy minister's household, which frequently included visitors or boarders. Though his father's circumstances were modest, his family tree on both sides included distinguished leaders of the Puritan commonwealth. Both his parents were ambitious for him. His father Timothy was a good, if rigorous, teacher of the classics, and Jonathan received his primary education at home. Timothy's letters home from travels reveal a compulsive worrier. Indeed, Jonathan's modern biographer calls Timothy

> a man careful and troubled about many things, one who forgot nothing and yet assumed that everyone else forgot everything continually, one who busied himself unnecessarily with the obligations of others and half enjoyed the self-imposed burden of details innumerable. . . . Instead of quieting childish fears he raised them, as though parental guidance consisted in advance notice of potential disaster.[2]

It is little wonder that Jonathan—precocious, brilliant, and anxious—sought solitude in swamp and woods. There he prayed, and he also observed the life around him. From these observations came his incisive essay on the habits of spiders, written in his twelfth or thirteenth year, which proud Timothy mailed to an English naturalist.[3] Before leaving for Yale College at age thirteen, Jonathan also wrote an essay called "On Colors," which showed he had somehow obtained and mastered information from Isaac Newton's *Opticks*.[4]

In college, in addition to the regular curriculum, young Jonathan read John Locke and began his own "Notes on the Mind." After reading Newton further he began "Notes on Natural Science." He might have become a brilliant naturalist and scientist, as did Benjamin Franklin, three years his junior; but his graduate studies coincided with the religious decision that pointed him in a different direction. He was tired of academic life, having been overburdened by those who admired his brilliance. At age twenty-one Edwards was senior tutor at Yale, instructing sixty students, and he was also effectively in charge of the college since it then had no president. He yearned to flee these vexations.

During this period, which he later called his time of conversion, Edwards recorded his self-improvement resolutions in a style common to the day. Young Ben Franklin kept a similar diary. Some entries show Jonathan's youthful vitality: "*Resolved,* To live with all my might, while I do live." Others show a growing genius enjoying his intellectual capacities: "*Resolved,* When I think of any Theorem in divinity to be solved, immediately to do what I can towards solving it, if circumstances do not hinder." Most entries, however, exhibit the self-punishment of an earnest young Puritan trying to make peace with his conscience and his God.

> *Resolved,* To endeavour to obtain for myself as much happiness, in the other world, as I possibly can, with all the power, might, vigour, and vehemence, *yea violence,* I am capable of, or can bring myself to exert, in any way that can be thought of.[5]

Though he was bursting with life and intellectual creativity, Edwards was also convinced that peace with God came through humble self-surrender. This he was determined to achieve, by force if necessary. On January 12, 1723, in New York City, he completed what he would later call his conversion with a classic resolution of Christian resignation: "Never, henceforward, till I die, to act as if I were any way my own, but entirely and altogether God's. . . . That no other end but religion, shall have any influence at all on any of my actions."[6]

These were the thoughts he permitted himself to express in his diary at the time. But 16 years later, after living through the Northampton revival, his recollections of that earlier time were transformed. In the later account his emphasis changed from dwelling upon resignation to remembering "inward, sweet delight in God and divine things . . . a sense of the glory of the Divine Being."[7] His memories were now sensuous. He even recalled how he had participated in that common exercise of adolescent Christians, meditating on the explicitly erotic images in the Biblical Canticles (Song of Songs) and applying them to his personal relationship with Christ:

> The whole book of Canticles used to be pleasant to me, and I used to be much in reading it, about that time; and found, from time to time, an inward sweetness, that would carry me away, in my contemplations . . . a kind of vision, or fixed ideas and imaginations, of being alone in the mountains, or some solitary wilderness, far from all mankind, sweetly conversing with Christ, and wrapt and swallowed up in God. The sense I had of divine things, would often of a sudden kindle up, as it were, a sweet burning in my heart; an ardor of soul, that I know not how to express.[8]

From his vantage of 1739, Edwards remembered how nature figured prominently in his meditations during the time of his conversion. He experienced intense sensory engagement with the natural world. He not only saw the world vividly, but he responded expressively with song:

> God's excellency, his wisdom, his purity and love, seemed to appear in every thing; in the sun, moon, and stars; in the clouds, and blue sky; in the grass, flowers, trees; in the water, and all nature; which used greatly to fix my mind. I often used to sit and view the moon for continuance; and in the day, spent much time in viewing the clouds and sky, to behold the sweet glory of God in these things; in the mean time, singing forth, with a low voice my contemplations of the Creator and Redeemer.[9]

Edwards' experience with God deepened and his trust grew; his delight in nature also increased. Former fears became joys. His reconciliation with God joined him more deeply to the world around him.

> Scarce any thing, among all the works of nature, was so sweet to me as thunder and lightning; formerly, nothing

had been so terrible to me. . . . I felt God, so to speak, at the first appearance of a thunder storm; and used to take the opportunity, at such times, to fix myself in order to view the clouds, and see the lightnings play, and hear the majestic and awful voice of God's thunder, which oftentimes was exceedingly entertaining, leading me to sweet contemplations of my great and glorious God. While thus engaged, it always seemed natural to me to sing, or chant for my meditations; or, to speak my thoughts in soliloquies with a singing voice.[10]

This is a moving description of mental and spiritual health: senses opening to one's surroundings, heart trusting the integrity of God and the world, and voice rising in heart-felt, responsive praise. What is striking is that none of this open, expressive spirit is apparent in the diary kept at the time. Indeed Edwards, looking back, remembered how blocked had been young Jonathan's emotions:

It used at that time to appear a great part of the happiness of heaven, that there the saints could express their love to Christ. It appeared to me a great clog and burden, that what I felt within, I could not express as I desired. The inward ardor of my soul, seemed to be hindered and pent up, and could not freely flame out as it would.[11]

From his youth onward, Edwards was a compulsive note-taker. But the experiences that he remembered in 1739 as the core of his youthful conversion were not the ones he selected at the time to enter in his diary. Something important had changed in the meantime. The youth at nineteen may indeed have felt those things which the man at thirty-six recalled. But at nineteen Jonathan could not reflect upon them. He could not write them down, nor could he fully accept them into his self-understanding. Edwards' early diary recorded the self-supervision of a divided spirit, not the joyful discovery of a whole person.

Later, it remained important to Edwards to identify this youthful period as his time of conversion, because that was the time he dedicated himself to God and took up the ministerial vocation. But I believe his real, personal awakening occurred as a consequence of the revival among his people in 1734. Edwards—ever shy, cool, and undemonstrative— needed to be surrounded by that emotional outpouring. Within it he could give himself permission to feel, and to let those feelings rise to consciousness. Supported by general excitement, he could taste his own sensuous relationships with God and the world. These personal benefits contributed to his vigor in defending the awakening. They help explain why, for the remainder of his life, Edwards meditated on the meaning of this revival. The awakening had saved him also.

Edwards needed cultural support in order to experience the depth of his own feelings, so he helped create that social context in the Northampton revival and in the Great Awakening which flowed from it. Many other people, less sophisticated than Edwards, but products of the same tradition of emotional restraint, also needed permission from an authority and support from a trusted group in order to acknowledge their feelings and to express themselves more openly. The intense Northampton revival was the first such event to break the cultural bonds of restraint and to support new, collective expression. Out of the depths of their need, people responded enthusiastically. This flame spread to other towns until the glowing heat created wildfire.

I believe that Edwards may have revealed the precise moment when all came together for him in a vision of beauty and peace, releasing his deepest feelings. The setting was the woods outside Northampton where, continuing the habit formed in childhood, he retreated regularly for peace of mind.

> Once, as I rode out into the woods for my health, in 1737, having alighted from my horse in a retired place, as my manner commonly has been, to walk for divine contemplation and prayer, I had a view that for me was extraordinary, of the glory of the Son of God, as Mediator between God and man, and his wonderful, great, full, pure and sweet grace and love, and meek and gentle condescension. This grace that appeared so calm and sweet, appeared also great above the heavens. The person of Christ appeared ineffably excellent with an excellency

> great enough to swallow up all thought and conception . . .
> which continued as near as I can judge, about an hour;
> which kept me the greater part of the time in a flood of
> tears, and weeping aloud. . . . I have, several other times,
> had views very much of the same nature, and which have
> had the same effects.[12]

Edwards could now cry, sing aloud, remember these things,
and write them down as significant to his life. He was alive,
by the grace of God, with the life he had given to his people
and received back from them.[13]

* * *

Another significant difference between the youth
Jonathan writing in his diary and the man Edwards preaching in the awakening was his marriage to Sarah Pierpont. At
nineteen Jonathan was already in love with Sarah, who was
pious, intelligent, and uncommonly beautiful. They married
after a year of his Northampton pastorate, when he was
twenty-three and she seventeen. By all accounts they were a
devoted couple throughout their years together. In this relationship Edwards tasted the beauties of intimacy.

Puritan piety, building on Paul's image in Ephesians,
saw marriage as a metaphor of the relationship between
Christ and the believer.[14] The erotic images of the Song of
Songs were also used, metaphorically, to express the delights of faith. Among New England Puritans this metaphor
for faith was developed by married men who had some experience of sexual ecstasy. Feminist historian Amanda
Porterfield observes,

> One of the most striking phenomena about the
> New England Puritans is that their greatest ministers
> and governors—Thomas Shepard, John Winthrop, Simon
> Bradstreet, Edward Taylor, and Jonathan Edwards, for
> example—loved their wives beyond measure. These men
> found their wives to be earthly representatives of God's
> beauty. For these men a loving wife was not only a model
> Christian but also an expression of the beauty of the
> world that pointed beyond itself to divine beauty. And

the enjoyment of God's beauty was the essence of Puritan spirituality.[15]

The marriage metaphor expressed the "experimental" expectation of Puritan piety. Puritans believed that receiving God's redeeming grace was a sensuous experience, and that knowing God face to face would be rapturous. Sexual delight might be a foretaste.

On the other hand, these relationships were held in hierarchy. A married woman was to subordinate herself to her husband. However, a couple must also subordinate their marriage—and the joys they shared within it—to the relationship that each partner had with God. Women were called to be twice submissive: to their husbands, and even more to their Lord. Men had to learn the contrasting roles of being strong leaders in the family, representing the Lord, and also being humble like women in their own relationship to God. A woman both pious and dutiful, such as Sarah Edwards, might take on a special religious significance to the men around her. In her daily deportment she exemplified the attitude which a man must carry toward God in his heart. Although this perception enriched the spiritual dimension of love toward such a woman, the love could also be dangerous if it became more important than one's loving relationship with God.

After Jonathan married Sarah, he knew his first experiences of sexual release. Surely this reinforced Edwards' growing intellectual commitment to the importance of the affections in the function of the human personality. Nevertheless, Edwards would likely have tempered his marital enjoyment with his conviction that joy in the Lord must always be the Christian's primary delight. Edwards' affirmation of human affectionate capacities—his psychology—was partially undermined by this rigorous hierarchical perspective. Because he was anxious that lesser goods remain subordinate to higher goods, he saw as idolatrous those earthly joys which became too intense or threatened to preoccupy his thoughts.

As a young married man, Edwards may have found himself in a "double-bind." He was deeply in love, discovering new sensations and feelings, and he was intellectually committed to the primacy of experience and affectionate expression for the healthy functioning of human personality. On the other hand, his keen Puritan conscience warned of danger if sensual enjoyment with Sarah threatened to compete with his direct, religious experience of God. Love for God was certainly central to Edwards' life. But was that love felt, experienced, and expressed with full emotional discharge? Any uncertainty here placed both his faith and his marriage under a cloud. Edwards, emotionally reticent, was not likely to find inward peace, assurance in faith, and ease with the joys of marriage, until he could fully discharge his feelings toward the Lord. For this, I believe, Edwards needed the awakening. His people, bound in the same culture and sometimes haunted in their own marital relations by similar doubts and fears, needed the awakening as well.

* * *

Even in the midst of the revival, there were limits to Edwards' expressiveness. Two of these limitations, common to his culture, would constrain the liberating impact of the Great Awakening: one was related to nature and one to the body.

Only in his private writings could Edwards portray the role that communion with nature played in his spiritual development. He failed to acknowledge the role of nature publicly, and he did not integrate experience with nature into his preaching. Only in his last years of life did he begin serious theological reflection on the earth and natural life.

Edwards had begun his intellectual pilgrimage as a precocious naturalist. As a young student he drew brilliant metaphors from nature. At Yale, for example, he expressed the philosophical idea of non-being with a simple but lucid parallel: "We must think of the same that the sleeping Rocks Dream and not till then shall we Get a Compleat idea of nothing."[16] Later, as a serious preacher, Edwards repressed this gift, failing to transcend the iconoclastic conventions of Puritan rhetoric that discouraged interpreting biblical truths through illustrations from life. A rare exception was his perversely effective use of the spider.

Thus, the integration of nature and faith recorded in Edwards' private writings was not communicated from his pulpit. Ola Elizabeth Winslow, Edwards' modern biographer, after reading hundreds of his sermons, confirms this lack:

> His figures of speech were almost strictly scriptural. When he needed briars and brambles, pastures and water brooks, a cloud the size of a man's hand, the high places of the forest, he took them from David and the Prophets and the Evangelists, as though he had never had a farm boyhood of his own, and had not every year of his life spent weeks in lonely horseback journeys through woods, breathtaking in their spring and autumn beauty. As a part of his own daily devotions, he was accustomed to going to the woods which bordered Northampton, tethering his horse and walking alone in meditation; yet so far as the thoughts he brought back had need to cloak themselves in images, he took them from the Bible, seldom from his own observations. [17]

Edwards' adherence to the abstract conventions of Puritan rhetoric hid from his hearers and obscured in his own reflections the deepest implication of his affectionate psychology: the ways natural experience and religious experience might nourish each other.

Edward's second limitation was an even more critical defect: he did not overcome alienation from his own body. Consequently, his religious psychology was also defective because he could not recognize the role of the body in human affections, including religious affections. Here he was a child of his time; though he was able to innovate in several areas, he could not transcend his culture in this area. He could not be an adequate pastor, therefore, to those who experienced physical distress as a result of the emotional trauma of revival. Though he would learn a great deal from his subsequent analysis of the emotions he observed in others during times of awakening, he refused to draw any inferences from their more tangible, physical symptoms. We will see how this block in his own perceptions damaged his ability to respond helpfully to his wife, Sarah, when she experienced intense physical distress after her own time of religious awakening.

Often weak and sickly, Edwards dragged his body through daily life as baggage to his keen mind. The affections he exalted were detached from their physical components.

12. *Sarah's Experience*

In 1741 and 1742 the Great Awakening was at its height, not just in New England but throughout the American colonies. Jonathan Edwards stood forward as its leading apologist. He was also trying to discriminate—to separate saving experience from the inconsequential and the harmful. In the fall of 1741 he addressed the academic community at Yale on "The Distinguishing Marks of a Work of the Spirit of God," his first attempt to give theological definition to the popular experiences. A year later Edwards prepared a more practical treatise "concerning the present revival of religion . . . and the way in which it ought to be acknowledged and promoted."[1] As the climax to that work he told, suitably disguised, the story of his wife's experience in January 1742.

Sarah was thirty-one years old then, the loving, competent wife of a famous preacher at the height of his controversial career. She had borne a healthy child every second year since their marriage, and was now raising seven children. (She would bear eleven children, all of whom survived childhood, a remarkable circumstance in that era.) That January she had an intense religious experience during a revival. At her husband's request, Sarah wrote a full account of this experience, one of few such reports from a layperson, and Edwards used her writing as the basis for his published version. Sarah's own version, which I will quote in this chapter, was finally published ninety years later in a biography of her husband.[2]

Sarah's remarkable narrative not only reveals the beauty in religious experience common during the awakening; it also reveals psychological difficulties which, given the constraints in her culture, were also commonly associated with revival. The same culture that supported emotional expression in a religious revival, remained anxious about such expression in the settings of daily life. Sarah's inhibition of such expression took its toll on her health.

Edwards had become convinced that the full flow of human feelings must be supported and encouraged, particularly in relation to God and the "things of religion." When he tried to distinguish valuable religious affections from the distracting emotions that accompanied a revival, Edwards became convinced that God can be truly known only if God is the direct object of enjoyment. God is not honored by ulterior motives. The experience of God is not enhanced by what we would recognize today as displaced emotions, when God is surrogate for other, unfulfilled longings. Edwards asked,

> How can that be true love of this excellent and lovely nature, which is not built on the foundation of its true loveliness? How can that be true love of beauty and brightness, which is not for beauty and brightness' sake?[3]

Interpreting Sarah's narrative requires some "psychohistory"—psychological interpretation based on historical record. This is an uncertain task, particularly when so little biographical information survives.[4] Her husband's version of Sarah's story, widely read for generations, became an American myth of faith and helped shape religious expectation within the evangelical tradition. An examination of Sarah's story may help us reform these expectations and isolate problems common to the tradition.

*   *   *

To bear so many children successfully, and to care for them along with her husband in a busy ministerial household, Sarah must have been a strong woman. Even in a strong person, childbirth and other demands might from time to time lead to depression. Introducing his disguised account, Edwards noted that during previous years "the person" of the narrative had been "often subject to melancholy, and at times almost overborne with it."[5] He speculated that this was due to "a vapory habit of body," suggesting a weaker constitution than we might infer from Sarah's successful motherhood.

We know nothing of Sarah's childhood, other than that she was the daughter of a distinguished New Haven preacher by his third wife. Girls in such households were trained to be both docile and spiritual, an upbringing which might stifle awareness of desires for personal expression. Legend has it that by age five Sarah exhibited "the life and power of religion, and that in a remarkable manner."[6] We may assume that, in addition to a good education, she was taught submission to God and was prepared for submission to a husband. At age thirteen she had a sweet, somewhat detached aspect which captivated Jonathan, then nineteen. He wrote at the time that God

> comes to her and fills her mind with exceeding sweet delight, and that she hardly cares for anything, except to meditate on him. . . . She is of a wonderful sweetness, calmness and universal benevolence of mind. . . . She loves to be alone, walking in the fields and groves, and seems to have someone invisible always conversing with her. . . .[7]

At the onset of adolescence, Sarah's self-image of Christian piety was surely reinforced by the admiration of her distinguished suitor. At seventeen she married New England's most brilliant young scholar and promising preacher. Since her husband was not gifted in the chores of daily life, Sarah managed their complex, busy household. His forceful character and public prominence strengthened the cultural pattern of male leadership and wifely assistance. When her husband was struck down by illness in middle life, she followed him to the grave in less than a year.

The story of Sarah's awakening, however, relates a distinctive moment when she was independent, when she was strong, and when she experienced herself deeply. It also tells of the terror these new feelings aroused. Sarah's story is the struggle between her freedom to delight in Christ and her fear of pleasurable expression.

Edwards was away for two weeks, and Sarah was required to host several guest ministers who were preaching a local revival. She began the account of her awakening by noting a rebuke from "Mr. Edwards" shortly before his departure. She was anxious for his approval. "This, I much disliked in myself, as arguing a want of a sufficient rest in God, and felt a disposition to fight against it, and look to God for his help." She also wished to feel less anxious about criticism from "the people of this town." When morning family prayers —led by the visiting Mr. Reynolds—were concluded, Sarah retired to private prayer during which she felt assurance of God's love. "Melted and overcome by the sweetness of this assurance, I fell into a great flow of tears, and could not forbear weeping aloud." Even the thought of criticism from her husband or townsfolk was undaunting: "if I were exposed to them both, they would seem comparatively nothing." She felt God gave her the strength she had asked for.[8]

With this confidence Sarah was able to handle a twinge of jealousy when she heard that "Mr. Buell," an unusually flamboyant but successful evangelist, was coming to Northampton to preach in her husband's pulpit. Intellectually, Buell was no match for her husband, but Sarah could accept the fact that God might "employ babes and sucklings to advance his kingdom." Indeed, she came to take a certain satisfaction in "the greater success attending his preaching, than had followed the preaching of Mr. Edwards immediately before he went to Leicester." Sarah's confident, positive feelings continued for several days, and her self-esteem was supported by her interaction with the several visiting ministers. When Mr. Buell brought friends after church for prayer in her home, she shared her strong feelings with the group. She recorded, "I continued to enjoy this intense, and lively and refreshing sense of Divine things, accompanied with strong emotions, for nearly an hour; after which, I experienced a delightful calm, and peace and rest in God, until I retired for the night."[9]

The company, particularly the visiting men, stimulated her. With her husband away, she also had the opportunity to be by herself at night in the privacy of her bedroom, where she could own her feelings. It was here, three nights later, that her joy came intensely to fulfillment. She met Christ and, without apparent physical symptoms, felt emotional ecstasy.

> That night, which was Thursday night, Jan. 28, was the sweetest night I ever had in my life. I never before, for so long a time together, enjoyed so much of the light, and rest and sweetness of heaven in my soul, but without the least agitation of body during the whole time. The great part of the night I lay awake, sometimes asleep, and sometimes between sleeping and waking. But all night I continued in a constant, clear and lively sense of the heavenly sweetness of Christ's excellent and transcendent love, of his nearness to me, and of my dearness to him; with an inexpressibly sweet calmness of soul in an entire rest in him. I seemed to myself to perceive a glow of divine love come down from the heart of Christ in heaven, into my heart, in a constant stream, like a stream or pencil of sweet light. At the same time, my heart and soul all flowed out in love to Christ; so that there seemed to be a constant flowing and reflowing of heavenly and divine love, from Christ's heart to mine; and I appeared to myself to float or swim, in these bright, sweet beams of the love of Christ, like the motes swimming in the beams of the sun, or the streams of his light which come in at the window.[10]

Here Sarah conveyed a full experience—clear sensations and strong emotions—not dream fantasies floating in the mind. The mildly erotic imagery, which was quite acceptable to Puritan sensibility, suggests the mobilizing of sexual energies that appropriately accompany intense experience. Sarah's beautiful encounter with Christ was a blessing which her Christian culture helped her to realize.

Sarah noted that she was "without the least agitation of body during the whole time." Here is the first hint of a problem that would become severe during the following days. Such complete blocking of physical expression was not healthy; and as Sarah shared her experience with others, she continued to resist physical contact. This pattern of intense feeling without physical outlet would become acutely burdensome.

The next morning, responding to a warm greeting from another visitor, Mr. Sheldon, Sarah poured out to him and others present the experience of the night. "So intense were my feelings, when speaking of these things, that I could not forbear rising up and leaping with joy and exultation. I felt at the same time an exceedingly strong and tender affection for the children of God, and realized, in a manner exceedingly sweet and ravishing, the meaning of Christ's prayer . . . 'That they all may be one.' "[11] Although loving energy flowed out to embrace those able to accept her experience, her physical movements were confined to "rising up and leaping," rather than touching those toward whom her feelings were flowing.

Sarah attended two church services that day, remaining in the church building between the services to talk with friends. Her tension must have been evident in her manner, for some of her friends expressed concern for her health. They did not know whether to support her or constrain her. Sarah picked up gossip about a friend who "had expressed her fears lest I should die before Mr. Edwards' return, and he should think the people had killed his wife; I told those who were present, that I chose to die in the way that was most agreeable to God's will."[12] The words, "chose to die," suggest that Sarah was indeed beginning to doubt that feelings so intense as hers could be expressed in this life. That night, when she was in bed, her thoughts were all of death. As days passed, Sarah's preoccupation with death deepened and acquired a distinctly masochistic quality.

Masochism is a type of neurosis that may result when the ego strives for pleasure but perceives the outer world is blocking these strivings. Because the masochist anticipates punishment, and doubts that intense pleasure can be experienced without pain, a masochistic person often seeks release with pain and dwells on the prospect of death. I surmise that Sarah's strong feelings had now awakened the repressive energy from her childhood training, and the anxiety of her friends may have reinforced it.

Despite her loving feelings toward others and her desire for contact, Sarah fantasized punishment. She feared rejection and imagined surviving cruelty passively, without complaint:

> When I arose on the morning of the Sabbath, I felt a love to all mankind, wholly peculiar in its strength and sweetness, far beyond all that I had ever felt before. The power of that love seemed to be inexpressible. I thought, if I were surrounded by enemies, who were venting their malice and cruelty upon me, in tormenting me, it would still be impossible that I should cherish any feelings towards them but those of love, and pity and ardent desires for their happiness. At the same time I thought, if I were cast off by my nearest and dearest friends, and if the feelings and conduct of my husband were to be changed from tenderness and affection, to extreme hatred and cruelty, and that every day, I could so rest in God, that it would not touch my heart, or diminish my happiness. I could still go on with alacrity in the performance of every act of duty, and my happiness remain undiminished and entire. 13

Two days later Sarah began to have fainting spells. These spells seemed to act out her heightened fear of expressing her feelings, her inner warfare between expression and repression. Her first seizure was accompanied by a fantasy of deliverance. "In the evening, these words, in the Penitential Cries,—'The Comforter is Come!'— were accompanied to my soul with such conscious certainty, and such intense joy, that immediately it took away my strength, and I was falling to the floor; when some of those who were near me caught me and held me up."14 Her fainting, which was always in the company of friends, recurred on several days. It brought her physical contact, although her friends became increasingly anxious.

The last vivid image in Sarah's spiritual narrative is a masochistic fantasy with overtones of sexual exhibition, a fantasy of escape to God. She chose to relate this fantasy one evening to several men who were to sleep in her house that night.

> I told him [Mr. Clark, present with Mr. Buell and
> two other men] that . . . I had asked myself when I lay
> down, How I should feel, if our house and all our property
> in it should be burnt up, and we should that night be
> turned out naked; whether I could cheerfully resign all to
> God; and whether I so saw that all was his, that I could
> fully consent to his will, in being deprived of it? and that I
> found, so far as I could judge, an entire resignation to his
> will, and felt that, if he should thus strip me of every thing,
> I had nothing to say, but should, I thought, have an entire
> calm and rest in God. [15]

When, in conversation with these ministers, Sarah
pictured herself naked and suffering, she was not only communicating her pain but was also unwittingly creating a sug-
gestive and uncomfortable situation for them all. She was
acting out her masochism.

*   *   *

Sarah's narrative reveals a troubled woman who could
not cope with her awakened feelings. She fantasized punishment and death as alternatives to living with feelings greater
than she could express.

Sarah had responded to the stimulation of the revival atmosphere at a time when she was challenged by her
husband's absence and when she had private space for meditation. Beginning this bittersweet pilgrimage by praying
for strength and self-esteem, she gained heightened self-
confidence. In this confidence she allowed herself emotional
awareness that led to an intense experience of love with
Christ. Sarah was able to recount this experience to friends
and share with them the symbolic phrases of Christian communion; yet when she felt her love and her need for them,
she could express herself neither in direct words nor in
physical contact.

The Great Awakening supported the expression of
feelings in a religious context. It did not give to Sarah, however, the help she needed to understand the physical energies
and even sexual desires that infused her emotions. Despite

the awakening, her culture did not give adequate support to human expression in daily life; indeed, her friends reinforced her repressive childhood training. Seeing their anxiety, Sarah panicked at the strength of her feelings, and then hid her panic from herself under a veneer of resignation. These conflicting pressures led to fainting in the company of others and to morbid meditations when she was alone. Her taste of joy turned sour.

For Sarah Edwards, "the heavenly sweetness of Christ's excellent and transcendent love" turned into a preoccupation with punishment and death. Something was wrong, deeply wrong, with the religious culture which shaped her life and helped her interpret her experience.

13. *The Body*

When Jonathan Edwards returned, Sarah was suffering. Nevertheless, her words of faith told him what he wanted to hear. Although he had once been an acute observer of natural phenomena, now he let the language of piety mask the emotional disorientation and physical pain of the woman he loved. He wrote a few months later that her "steadfastness and constancy has remained through great outward changes and trials; such as times of the most extreme pain, and apparent hazard of immediate death." Instead of seeing in her distress a warning, Edwards accepted Sarah's account as vindication of his confidence in the awakening. When he concluded his disguised version of Sarah's story, he exulted in the teeth of his critics.

> Now if such things are enthusiasm, and the fruits of a distempered brain, let my brain be evermore possessed of that happy distemper! If this be distraction, I pray God that the world of mankind may be all seized with this benign, meek, beatifical, glorious distraction![1]

A few pages before Edwards' account of Sarah's experience, he gave a disclaimer that helps explain why he was blind to inferences from her physical condition. Critics of the Great Awakening had charged that many people suffered physical trauma as part of their revival experience. Edwards maintained that even if there were such trauma, it would not detract from the spiritual integrity of the experience. He vehemently dissociated himself from any responsibility for physical consequences:

> Scripture rules respect the state of the mind, and per-

> sons' moral conduct, and voluntary behavior, and not the
> physical state of the body. The design of the Scripture is
> to teach us divinity, and not physic and anatomy.
> Ministers are made the watchmen of men's souls, and not
> their bodies; and therefore the great rule which God has
> committed into their hands is to make them divines, and
> not physicians.

If Christ had wished ministers to be physicians, Edwards
lamely concluded, he would have included with the Gospels a
book of anatomy and medicine![2]

Here the tragic limitation to Edwards' leadership of
the Great Awakening is revealed. Although he transcended
the classic separation of reason, will, and emotions, insisting
properly that affections were at the core of human experience
and therefore at the heart of the human relationship with
God, he could not transcend the classic separation of mind
from body.

Where others had talked of bodily passions, Edwards
promoted affections to a prominent seat in the soul. However,
he could not complete this conceptual reformation and unite
the human personality—body and mind; matter and soul;
emotions, reason, will, and expression—into one. Instead, like
Descartes, Edwards imagined a mechanical, one-way relationship between mind and body. Though the affections and
other mental processes affected the whole person, the mind
was not equally vulnerable. It governed the body but was not
subject to it:

> Such is our nature, and such are the laws of the union of
> soul and body, that the mind can have no lively or vigorous
> exercise, without some effect upon the body. So subject is
> the body to the mind, and so much do its fluids, especially
> the animal spirits, attend the motions and exercises of the
> mind, that there can't be so much as an intense thought,
> without an effect upon them. Yea, 'tis questionable, whether
> an embodied soul ever so much as thinks one thought, or
> has any exercise at all, but that there is some correspond-
> ing motion or alteration of motion, in some degree, of the
> fluids, in some part of the body.[3]

In his account of Sarah's experience, Edwards noted several occasions when religious emotions had overwhelmed her "so as sometimes to take away the bodily strength." His explanation for these physical disabilities resulting from religious experience was that "the joy of soul has been too great for the body."[4]

Edwards had made a major advance in psychological understanding when he integrated the will and reason into the affections, imagining a more unified personality. Since he could not integrate body with mind, however, the usefulness of his insight was undermined. He did not recognize mutual interactions between feelings and physical conditions. To understand a person's feelings and to appraise emotional health, Edwards depended only upon the words the person chose to employ. Physical well-being was not relevant.

Therefore, for Edwards, emotions remained captive to ideology, and feelings were buried in rhetoric. With all its ability to wrap feelings in images, the head remained in control, interpreting the affections. Surely Edwards must have felt the pain of this woman he loved most dearly, but unfortunately he could respond only to her profession of faith.

* * *

"If you have ears, then hear." According to the current consensus among biblical scholars, Jesus and the Hebrew tradition behind him understood a human being to be a unified psychophysical organism, breathing the breath of life given by God. Jesus presumed that when we are healthy, we are not divided or layered; and this same notion appears in the Old Testament. This integrated perspective was lost when the Christian church absorbed psychological categories of the ancient Greeks, who sharply distinguished soul from body, and consequently it was veiled from Edwards' sight by millennia of alternative ideology.

Modern Christians, again conscious of this biblical perspective, may acknowledge human integrity and embrace all our personal and social capabilities. Human experience is rooted in the tangible characteristics of our being: our muscles, bones, organs, and breath, as well as our senses, nerves, glands, and brain tissue. All these characteristics contribute to our interaction with the range of life beyond us: with other persons and human culture, with the many facets of natural life, and with the Lord.

When we are aware of experience, when we are self-conscious, we have the experience of *mind*—our name for consciousness and reflective capacities. *Mind* and *brain* are not interchangeable concepts, for mind's awareness involves more than brain cells; it includes more from beneath the skin and from outside our skin as well. Reflective experience comprises both sensations and emotions, integrating a variety of organs. In our most engaging experience we reach beyond the boundaries of our flesh to incorporate a creative selection from our culture and environment into our identity. I summon ideas, values, landscapes, persons—even an image of God—to fashion myself.

Through what Edwards termed "affections" and some modern theories call *eros*, the self comes vividly to life. As noted in a previous chapter, this concept of self does not separate the subject from one's environment or one's culture, any more than it separates the mind from body and emotions. The self is a continually creative interplay of the full organism with its total environment.[5] A healthy person is a complex ecology.

Two common errors result from isolating the mind. Skeptics, who denigrate religious experience, suggest it is only in the mind, in order to deny God. Many religious people, additionally, make the error of assuming that while human experience of God requires the mind, or soul, it does not require the body and our full complex of responsive organs. This denigrates our flesh and maligns the God who fashioned us to be a creative unity. Edwards resisted associating "divinity" with "physic and anatomy." Nevertheless, the two must be joined.[6]

Religious experiences, like other intense experiences,

may at times be physically overwhelming. Life and growth may require periods of debilitating struggle. Both the physical and psychological components, however, are relevant to religious experience and to the quality of life valued in the biblical tradition. Indeed, body and psyche are within religious experience. They are neither just a context, nor a consequence. Debility may be tolerated on the path to wholeness, but it must not be excused as irrelevant.

When we affirm the unity of the human personality, then Edwards' principal conclusion concerning religious affections takes on fresh relevance. At the center of his analysis he rejected all displacement. Genuine affection is what it appears to be, but religious affections derived from other motives are not genuine. Faith cannot be a masquerade, for as Edwards himself said, "How can that be true love of beauty and brightness, which is not for beauty and brightness' sake?"[7]

Our knowledge of God, our love for God, and our resonance with God's beauty relate, therefore, to our psychic integrity and our capacity for direct experience. Stopped ears and blocked emotions do not prepare us to meet God. More insidiously, desires blocked in daily life, and then displaced onto a religious object may flare intensely, but they ultimately cloud our experience of God because they are about something else. If we wish to see God clearly we must run the risks of wholeness. The way to the Lord includes repairing the damage from daily life.

> If, when you are bringing your gift to the altar, you suddenly remember that your brother has a grievance against you, leave your gift where it is before the altar. First go and make your peace with your brother, and only then come back and offer your gift. (Matthew 5:23–24, NEB)

Jesus' suggestion also applies when it is my own grievance I remember—my anger or blocked desire. I need to know my common feelings and clarify my everyday relationships on my way to the Lord.

*   *   *

Edwards claimed that "Ministers are made the watchmen of men's souls, and not their bodies." One reason he avoided responsibility for the impact of the awakening upon physical welfare was that he was burdened with an exaggerated sense of his responsibility for the welfare of the spirit. Here is another misunderstanding of the role of Christian ministers, universal in Edwards' day and common in our own. As a "divine," Edwards felt responsible to understand and interpret the way of salvation. He believed he must discover where the spiritual interests of his people lay, and he assumed the duty to guide them authoritatively. This perspective made it more difficult for Edwards to learn from experience. He could not treat his psychological experiment in rhetoric as though it were, indeed, an experiment. He had to be sure, in advance, that it was truth, for he could not solicit feedback. Burdened with duty and anxiety, he found it hard to respect the idiosyncrasies of individual development.

Yet people did not believe they had been awakened in order to be watched and led: they felt they were awakened to be free. They now had experience of God with their own senses. As the intensity of their experience gave them confidence in themselves, they claimed more of the gospel than ministers were willing to yield. Edwards imagined that the outpouring of God's Spirit would make it possible to recreate the mythic piety of his Puritan ancestors within a newly disciplined, holy church. He was mistaken. The wine of mass awakening was truly new. When Edwards tried to pour it into century-old bottles, the bottles broke.

In 1744, as the Great Awakening was subsiding, it was discovered that Northampton adolescents had been passing a midwife's manual among themselves to enjoy the anatomical drawings and descriptions of childbirth. Here was natural adolescent curiosity, a vulgar equivalent of young Jonathan's own enjoyment of the Song of Songs. But the parallel escaped Edwards. He had already been under attack from conservative Boston clergy; he was now a victim of his anxiety to assure that Northampton, first town of the awakening, should maintain exemplary piety. He officiously constituted an elaborate church inquest and trial that involved children from most town families, either as the accused or as witnesses, and left all with a bad taste and a bitter memory. He had learned no tolerance of youthful energy and sexual curiosity from his new psychology.

Northampton, like the other awakened villages, gradually returned to a small-town normality which did not resemble "New Jerusalem." People were becoming irritable toward the minister who had been too prominent in their lives, and bickering developed concerning Edwards' salary and other matters. Edwards decided to strike at the root of a cluster of such problems, and purify the church. In 1748 he announced he would no longer accept applicants for church membership who could not profess a sincere belief in their own "renovation of heart." With one blow he would strike down the compromise that had opened communion to children of believers—the system his grandfather had fashioned in Northampton to keep a church alive when fervor receded, and which had become common practice throughout New England. Church membership would now be reserved for the truly awakened.

But the Great Awakening had changed things. Revived congregations throughout the colonies were now feisty. In New England, where Puritan churches had rarely exercised their congregational prerogative to dismiss ministers, many were now firing preachers of whom they grew tired. In Northampton Joseph Hawley, the son of Edwards' uncle who had cut his own throat following the revival of 1734, led the opposition. He was joined by others, now young adults, who had been embarrassed over the midwife manual inquiry, and eventually by the majority of church and town. They had had enough of Edwards. A protracted struggle ensued, during which Edwards irritated the people even more by remaining impassive: he would propound theology, but he would not engage with their anger. Indeed he corked his feelings, even in private. His biographer notes that "Jonathan Edwards' own journal of the whole affair, which runs to ninety printed pages, has the impersonality of an official record."[8] The congregation and town, voting together, dismissed Edwards from his pulpit in 1750.

He accepted an appointment to the frontier settlement of Stockbridge, Massachusetts, where, in a poorly conceived enterprise under an absentee board, he directed a tiny mission to the Housatunnock Indians. Here, teaching and exhorting those who could understand only the simplest English, crowded into a small house with Sarah, their eleven children, and sometimes garrisoned troops, Edwards found peace. The Housatunnock liked him for his straight manner and dependable concern. He found time in the seven Stockbridge years for a vast outpouring of writing, beginning with tracts that expressed his final rebuttal in all the controversies in which he had become embroiled. Gradually moving to more creative thinking, he produced his definitive *Freedom of the Will*, followed by *The Nature of True Virtue* and *Concerning the End for Which God Created the World*. He filled his notebooks with thoughts for projects not completed: these contain some of Edwards' most exciting insights.

When the College of New Jersey (now Princeton) invited Edwards to become its President, he argued against leaving the peace he had fashioned for himself in the wilderness. The problems of academic administration he remembered with distaste from his youth, and he knew his health was poor. Reluctantly, pressed by many admirers, he accepted the duty. When Edwards arrived in Princeton, he entered a smallpox epidemic which officials were trying to control with the new Pasteur vaccine. As a scientist, Edwards understood how important this procedure might be, and he determined to set a good example. Asserting mind over body, he did not give a voice to his own frame. He was too tired and sickly, however, to withstand the immunizing dose. Edwards died on March 22, 1758, at age fifty-four.

Part IV.

Identity

In 1971, when I was thirty-six, I fled from my Christian ministry in West Virginia and from my cross-country efforts to control strip mining for coal, as well as from my wife and three sons. Each of these relationships had become overwhelming. I hid out in Boulder, Colorado, lonely, guilty, and anxious. I asked God for help and received help of a different sort than I expected. I wished for a sense of God's comforting presence, but what I experienced—so clearly that I can still recall the taste—was God's reticence, God's deliberate restraint. I did not feel abandoned but confirmed; I was "on my own," without inspiring instructions.

None of my theological mentors spoke helpfully to me now—except Martin Luther. One of his sayings I wrote large on a sheet of newsprint and hung it on the bare wall of my rented room:

> [When] Christ comes and talks to you as if to a sinner and tortures you like Moses: "What have you done?"—slay him to death. But when he talks to you as God does, and as a savior, prick up both ears.[1]

I set aside my coherent images of God and the world, and with them my prior understanding of who I was and where I was going. I lived for a time on the strength of one simple conviction: I needed to find myself, my feelings, and my capacities. If I did not, I would be of no use to myself, my Lord, my family, or the world. I trusted that God would rather have me whole than have me submissive.

For several months I leaned heavily upon both a lover and a psychotherapist: I remain grateful to them. I felt sensations and expressed emotions I had once been afraid to own. I had to learn to walk: to find my own ground, carry my own weight, and move in my own direction. Deliberately restraining my compulsion to supervise myself, I allowed my capacities to grow in trust that when I was whole I would not be lost. It took several years before new physical skills and emotional experiences joined with faith and insight to confirm my identity and renew my sense of vocation.

I now call that particular experience the "elusive presence" of God—borrowing the title from Samuel Terrien's biblical study of God's revealing and hiding.[2] God creates other lives and takes delight in our independence and our self-awareness, for these are qualities which can make life's interrelationships more complex and beautiful. God supports our self-consciousness with periods of withdrawal as well as moments of revelation. When we trust God, the withdrawal, like the revelation, can communicate God's beauty.

The following chapters define the human response to God's beauty with the term *identity,* rather than the more traditional term, *faith.* The word *identity,* popularized by Erik Erikson, is more useful in this context because it highlights our complex interactions with our environment—both nature and culture—in the discovery of our faith and our self.

Here we reach the kernel of Jonathan Edwards' theological insight: a person is made whole through a sensuous awakening to the beauty of the Lord. Wholeness differs from the anxious intensity which may characterize an insecure identity. Stepping beyond Edwards, I suggest that the beauty of the Lord undergirds the existence of God so that even in the modern, skeptical environment, we may draw confidence from our experience of God's beauty.

14. God's Enjoyment

Jonathan Edwards stressed that God is uniquely "sensible." By this he did not mean that God is prudent, but that the Lord as revealed in the Bible is able to see, to feel, and to respond to the world. God, uniquely perceptive, can see in the human heart what we ourselves fear to know. The Lord hears the faint cries of the helpless widow or orphan, and feels towering indignation. Expressing rage like a whirlwind, the Lord then feels such compassion as to turn the tide of history. God is even moved to self-sacrifice—a Christian perception that staggers the human imagination. "As He is more sensible," Edwards reflected, "so He is, as I may express it, more voluntary than created minds. He acts more of Himself, infinitely more purely active."[1] The Lord is distinctively alive.

Within biblical stories, God's vitality is rarely in doubt; the challenge is to understand the coherence in this abundance of divine activity. Theologies, human efforts to understand God, are often built around central concepts that attempt to convey this coherence. One such unifying image in the Bible is the righteousness of God, which expresses the interplay of God's justice and mercy. Another unifying image is God's love; it conveys the self-giving which Jesus revealed from the heart of God. Like Jonathan Edwards, I am developing a less common focal image: the beauty of the Lord. Edwards interpreted God's righteousness, so awesome yet so attractive, as God's moral beauty. He infused this idea of beauty with the Christian image of the love of God, developing an understanding of beauty which surpassed traditional philosophical, psychological, and aesthetic reflection.

Beauty reaches to engage the observer. At the core the Lord is beautiful, for the heart of God is not self-contained but expressive. As God's righteousness shines forth, God creates, loves, and establishes relationships. The language of Christian philosophy has often not done justice to God's striking sensibility, portrayed in the Bible. As the Christian church matured in the Roman Empire, and Christian philosophers learned to think within the categories of Greek thought, a tension developed between this expressive biblical imagery and the more sophisticated, dispassionate terms of Greek reflection. In competition with Platonists and Stoics, Christian philosophers wished to stress that their God was omnipotent, eternal, all-knowing, perfect, unchanging, and self-sufficient. These concepts implied a God who was majestic, yet more remote. In practice, Christian piety came to identify this remote majesty with God the Father, while the images of God the Son, Mary, and the saints conveyed some of the expressive, engaging aspects of the biblical understanding of God.

When I came to understand Jonathan Edwards' emphasis on the beauty of God, I felt that Edwards bridged the gap between biblical and philosophical perspectives in a particularly helpful way. He asserted that "God is a communicating being" and again that "It is God's essence to incline to communicate Himself."[2] When Edwards thought about how God spoke so joyfully through the angels to announce the birth of Jesus, he concluded that God's desire to communicate did not derive "from any want or deficiency in God that he should stand in need of any other, but from his infinite fulness . . . which doth as it were overflow to the creature."[3]

When he stated that "beauty" was fundamental to God's nature and God's very being, Edwards chose a term from philosophical and aesthetic reflection to convey the expressiveness of the biblical Lord. Beauty shines forth. Locating beauty at the heart of God, assuming it to be God's most fundamental characteristic, changes our thought about God. If beauty is the heart of God, then God's giving forth, God's radiance, is more fundamental to the nature of the Lord than self-sufficiency. To state this in philosophical terms: Edwards modified the notion of "being itself" with the notion of beauty. He said that being is beautiful: that is, being itself has a tendency to communicate. This interpretation transforms a static philosophical notion into something active.[4]

* * *

The creation of the world, therefore, was not incidental, but flowed naturally from God's character—an appropriate manifestation of God's beauty. In his theology of creation Edwards avoided the extreme objectification of nature common in modern Western thought. He refused to reduce nature to a mere thing. Things are subject to human manipulation; they become property; they lack vitality and inherent value.

Rather than use the common Christian expression that God created the world *ex nihilo,* from nothing, Edwards preferred to say that God created the world *ad extra,* from God's overflowing abundance. The traditional expression protected Christian thought from pantheistic inferences that nature and God shared the same substance. It was also a corrective to dualistic notions, common in other religions, that God worked with recalcitrant materials to form a world compromised between good and evil. Although the notion of *ex nihilo* protected God's integrity and sovereignty, it did not express the moral connection between God and the world which is, from a biblical perspective, most important. Edwards wished to emphasize this moral relationship:

> As there is an infinite fulness of all possible good in God—a fulness of every perfection, of all excellency and beauty, and of infinite happiness—and as this fulness is capable of communication, or emanation *ad extra;* so it seems a thing amiable and valuable in itself that this infinite fountain of good should send forth abundant streams.[5]

In other words, God's beauty—righteousness, sensibility, creativity—is the heart of God's being. The creation of the world expresses God's fundamental character. Edwards declared, "If the world had not been created, these attributes never would have had any *exercise*."[6] Furthermore, he emphasized,

> The glory of God is the shining forth of His perfections. The world was created that they might shine forth—that is, that they might be communicated.[7]

The world is a basic expression of God's beauty. It is not an accidental or arbitrary creation; therefore the character and quality of the world reflect the character of God. Of course, our experience of the world is a fallen experience: human nature, human culture, and the environments under human dominion all exhibit broken relationships.[8] Because relationships with God, with other persons, and with nature are clouded by our sinfulness, it is not a simple matter to draw inferences concerning the character of God from our perception of nature. Edwards proposed no "natural theology," no reasonable reading of God's character from the face of the world. However, as our experience of God's beauty draws us to a new sense of life—restoring something of our taste for right relationships—we can indeed begin to sense the beauty of God through nature as well.

It is delightful to create. Beauty affects the creator as well as the creature. In Proverbs, where there is a poetic attempt to convey God's creative joy, God's self-awareness is personified as Wisdom, who sings of her enthusiasm.

> When he set the heavens in their place I was there,
> when he girdled the ocean with the horizon,
> when he fixed the canopy of clouds overhead
> and set the springs of ocean firm in their place,
> when he prescribed its limits for the sea
> and knit together earth's foundations.
> Then I was at his side each day,
> his darling and delight,
> playing in his presence continually,
> playing on the earth, when he had finished it,
> while my delight was in mankind.
>   (Proverbs 8:27–31, NEB)

Beauty is realized in creativity because it is expressive, not static. Such expressiveness unites the being of God with the goodness of God. As God "delights in glorifying himself," Edwards affirmed, it is "beautiful that infinite brightness and glory should shine forth"; thus "God delights in communicating his happiness to the creature," and in doing so God "enjoys himself."[9]

The expression of beauty is completed when there is a response, or an interplay between the creator and the created. Psalm 65 conveys the beauty of nature's responsiveness to God's goodness, as seen by people who depend upon this life-giving interaction:

> Thou visitest the earth and waterest it,
>> thou greatly enrichest it;
> the river of God is full of water,
>> thou providest their grain,
>> for so thou hast prepared it.
> Thou waterest its furrows abundantly,
>> settling its ridges,
> softening it with showers,
>> and blessing its growth.
> Thou crownest the year with thy bounty;
>> the tracks of thy chariot drip with fatness.
> The pastures of the wilderness drip,
>> and the hills gird themselves with joy;
> The meadows clothe themselves with flocks,
>> the valleys deck themselves with grain,
>> they shout and sing together for joy.
>> (Psalm 65:9–13, RSV)

Edwards concluded that the greatest beauty is in the act of *beautifying*—bringing others to fulfillment. The beauty of God, not a self-contained perfection, bursts forth into creativity. Now that sin has corrupted relationships and damaged creation, beauty is particularly evident in God's work to restore the world. The greatest beauty occurs when God reaches to rescue the fallen, opens human hearts to believe, and gives hope of final communion among all creatures. If beauty characterizes God's being, then God is most majestic when most engaged. The image of God in Christ suffering on the cross for the world does not compromise God's perfection, but reveals it. God is most glorified in the work of redemption.

* * *

All of God's creation, not just humanity, must be kept in view. Just as there is more to the beauty of the world than human welfare, so there is more to be seen in God's beauty than benevolence toward humanity alone. The biblical story of creation illustrates this truth. As the Genesis narrative unfolds, day by day, we see God's delight in how many different things come to life: "The earth yielded fresh growth, plants bearing seed according to their kind and trees bearing fruit each with seed according to its kind; and God saw that it was good" (Genesis 1:12, NEB). God's satisfaction at the end of the sixth day, after animals and humans were created, does not focus on the man and woman but embraces the whole: "And God saw every thing that [God] had made, and, behold, it was very good" (Genesis 1:31, KJV, alt.).

On the seventh day God rested to enjoy this great work in communion with "heaven and earth" and "all their mighty throng" (Genesis 2:1, NEB). This full communion expresses creation's purpose.[10] As theologian Jürgen Moltmann observed,

> The human being is certainly the living thing with the highest development known to us. But "the crown of creation" is God's sabbath. It is for this that human beings are created—for the feast of creation, which praises the eternal, inexhaustible God, and in this hymn of praise experiences and expresses its own joy. The enduring meaning of human existence lies in its *participation* in this joyful paean of God's creation. This song of praise was sung *before* the appearance of human beings, is sung *outside* the sphere of human beings, and will be sung even *after* human beings have—perhaps —disappeared from this planet. . . . The human being is not the meaning and purpose of the world.[11]

Many things which happen in this world are good even though they do not serve human interests. I explored this idea in the previous book of this series concerning John

Muir, America's first protector of wilderness. As a geologist Muir understood how the lush natural landscapes which humans love have been developed with the help of earthquakes and other violent manifestations of nature which humans tend to fear. He challenged Christians to transcend the limits of a humanocentric perspective. God does many gracious things which may not have humanity in view. Part of knowing the beauty of the Lord is breaking free from species-selfishness to rejoice in benefits to the rest of creation.

Even death may be seen as part of the beauty of God's creation, though it transcends our personal interest, and an appreciation of ecological values may help quiet our fear of death. Muir marveled that "We read our Bibles and remain fearful and uncomfortable amid Nature's loving destructions, her beautiful deaths."[12] Untimely death, unjust death, death which cuts off a life before it could know fulfillment—certainly these are tragic; but death itself is neither an aberration nor a punishment. Through death we make room for others, including members of other species; this is essential to the ecology of life. Christian attitude toward death is one of the building blocks of faith which needs to be inspected and reset. *Fear* of death is our enemy, more than death itself. When we learn to love all of life we may be able to sing with Francis of Assisi,

> Be praised, my Lord, for our Sister Bodily Death,
> From whom none can escape that has drawn breath.[13]

Although beauty is a vital quality of relationships, it is not a substitute for the objects of our relationships, those to whom it points. The beauty in religious experience may not properly be taken as a substitute for God, nor should the beauty in experience of nature lead us away from the objects of that experience. John Muir illustrated the first of these errors when he wrote, "Oh the infinite abundance and universality of Beauty. Beauty is God. What shall we say of God that we may not say of Beauty."[14] It is appropriate to say

"God is beauty," a statement that parallels biblical affirmations that "God is spirit" and "God is love," as well as Jesus' proclamation, "I am the way, the truth, and the life" (John 4:24, RSV; 1 John 4:8, KJV; John 14:6, KJV). However, it is not biblically correct to reverse the terms, to say "Spirit is God," "Love is God" or "Beauty is God." God is not just a quality in relationships, but a distinct, vital, complex personality. Although well-chosen words may help us know God, no word can encompass God, much less replace the Lord.

Profound experience of natural beauty may tempt one to the second error I mentioned, substituting one's beautiful experience for the things which aroused the experience. A mystical experience that glows while both the knowing subject and the objects of experience recede may suggest that value lies in the beauty, not in the thing. I do not believe this is a biblical understanding. Yet the Lord delights in creating other lives—lives with distinctiveness and individuality. God's creativity is manifest when each flower, rock, tree, and person shines with its own vitality, yet depends upon all and contributes to all in an ecology of life. John Muir, in a balanced observation, described the experience of touching the mystical core of beauty and returning from it to engage with living things. When observation of nature builds understanding, he wrote,

> the tendency is to unification. We at once find ourselves among eternities, infinitudes, and scarce know whether to be happy in the sublime simplicity of radical causes and origins or whether to be sorry on losing the beautiful fragments which we thought perfect and primary absolute units; but as we study and mingle with nature more, the pain caused by the melting of all beauties into one First Beauty disappears, because, after their first baptismal submergence in fountain God, they go again washed and clean into their individualisms, more clearly defined than ever, unified yet separate.[15]

Edwards, whose philosophical disposition was hierarchical and Platonic, described God as "the head of the universal system of existence; the foundation and fountain of all being and all beauty."[16] Roland Delattre observed that "To come to a knowledge of God is identical for Edwards with coming to see things as they are."[17] These statements remain sound if we replace Edwards' Christian Platonism with an ecological perspective, as I have done in this theology. The natural world expresses God because it has emerged, creatively and deliberately, from the character of the Lord. The beauties of the earth are truly expressions of the beauty of God.

However, it would not be true to reverse the terms and say that if we simply "see things as they are" we will "come to a knowledge of God." Creation expresses God, but neither exhausts nor limits God; God cannot be defined from creation. As we experience God we may grasp, with joyful insight, relationships between our Lord and the world we see around us. Indeed, we are so deeply imbedded in both nature and culture that we cannot know God apart from relationships with the world around us. Nevertheless, the biblical Lord remains a distinct Personality beyound nature and culture. When we glimpse the Lord's beauty, then we see both nature and culture in a new light.

* * *

Thinking about beauty in this way has led me to an additional insight: *the beauty of the Lord undergirds the existence of God.* The metaphysical quality, existence, does not precede the moral quality, beauty. God's being flows from the Lord's beauty. As Edwards affirmed, "God is God, and distinguished from all other beings, and exalted above 'em, chiefly by his divine beauty." [18]

Traditional religious philosophy sought first to establish God's existence and then to derive from that existence insight into God's character. Since modern minds often flounder on the first point, God's existence, we may despair entirely of the second. I suggest the reverse approach: begin with God's character, because moral character is more fundamental to our experience of God than metaphysical existence. In the biblical experience God's physical presence is elusive, but God's moral presence is demanding. While the traditional philosophical approach creates a speculative relationship with God, the alternative route which I suggest may lead to a moral relationship that affects one's life. Only within such a relationship do questions of the "being" or "existence" of God truly matter. When they do matter, the moral quality of the relationship provides part of the answer to those concerns.[19]

Since God is distinguished by divine beauty, so it is the Lord's character to be in relationship. This biblical understanding tempers philosophical anxiety with the joy of experience. It does not detract from the Lord to be self-giving, for God's relation to the world is not condescending, but vital and enthusiastic. The function of the Holy Spirit, Edwards suggests, is "to give all things their sweetness and beauty."[20] The greatest delight is in the act of beautifying; thus, "God delights in communicating his happiness to the creature . . . and so enjoys himself."[21]

15. *Experience of the Lord*

Experience of the Lord is elusive, yet morally compelling. We are not granted clear sense perceptions, such as the sight of an idol or a word heard through a loudspeaker. Biblical accounts emphasize the experience of the Lord as physically ambiguous. The "face" of God remained hidden, and one saw, at best, only the consequences of God's passing. Therefore our own experience of the Lord is likely to be one of "being known" as much as "knowing." After the Lord passes, what remains is not so much a clear image of another as change in oneself.

However ambivalent its sensory components, the experience of God is emotionally intense. When Jonathan Edwards described his religious experience, the object was mysterious, but the feeling of presence was vivid. "Holiness . . . appeared to me to be of a sweet, pleasant, charming, serene, calm nature, which brought an inexpressible purity, brightness, peacefulness, and ravishment to the soul. . . . It made the soul like a field or garden of God, with all manner of pleasant flowers."[1] Characteristically, experience of the Lord is liberating. It cleanses, opens feelings, integrates understanding, and releases energy. Conveying a sense of direction, it invites commitment: "Here am I; send me" (Isaiah 6:8, KJV). In this meeting the human personality comes to life, so that we are neither overwhelmed, nor destroyed.

" 'Tis improper to say," Edwards argued, "that our love to God is superior to our general capacity of delighting in anything."[2] Here there is a double insight. First, the Lord engages with our senses and emotional capacities; God does

not replace them with new facilities. Second, the quality of
these human capabilities influences the content of religious
encounter. Helping people free their feeling capacities may
assist their saving experience.

Christian theology has sometimes protected religious
experience from analysis by emphasizing its distinctiveness
rather than affirming its continuity with the rest of human
experience. The Calvinist tradition, to which Edwards was
loyal, rejected any suggestion that one could ascend from normal human experience toward an experience with God, like
climbing a ladder. So there was a potential theological diffi-
culty when Edwards realized that in meeting God we use the
same senses, emotional capacities and reflective abilities we
employ in daily life. Nevertheless, he was able to clarify rea-
sonably well how experience with God differs from other
human experience, while he also defended human psychological integrity.

Meeting God is distinctive in that the object of the
experience is unique. The sensual quality of experience with
God transcends any imagination we have of it, "as the sweet
taste of honey is diverse from the ideas men get of honey by
only looking on it, and feeling of it." God's beauty is more
potent than other beauties; while our knowledge of God
depends upon ordinary human senses, emotions, and intuition, they are so stimulated in this encounter that they seem
new. "Hence the work of the Spirit of God in regeneration,"
Edwards observed, "is often in Scripture compared to . . .
unstopping the ears of the deaf, and opening the eyes of them
that were born blind."[3]

Meeting God opens sensuous capacities. Our own
insensibility is replaced by awareness, so that our ears are no
longer "dull of hearing." When persons have experienced God,
their eyes are no longer held shut:

> *to avoid using their eyes to see, their ears to hear,*
> *their heart to understand,*
> *changing their ways and being healed by me.*
> (Matthew 13:15, JB)

We can be sure that God does not set human capabilities aside, because the Lord seeks an expressive relationship with us, not a repressive one. Edwards affirmed that the mental capacities are also stimulated when "beauty and sweetness . . . draws on the faculties" and stimulates the mind so that "reason itself is under far greater advantages . . . free of darkness and delusion."[4]

When society supports personal expressiveness this encourages religious feelings as well. Although in Puritan society shame and fear often inhibited the public display of emotion, during the Great Awakening it was acceptable to weep, to shout, to jump. The awakening stimulated popular imagination and provided social support for emotional release. It was acceptable to be afraid and to reveal it; anxiety was not locked below the level of consciousness. One was allowed to be joyful, even to express ecstasy, in the company of neighbors. This social permission for emotional expression encouraged beautiful meetings with the Lord. Edwards defended the awakening, in spite of its apparent excesses and dangers, because it helped people experience the love of God. Faced with weakened social controls and a spreading emotional instability, he nevertheless insisted that the "enthusiasm" be tolerated.

Edwards had been possessed by that paradoxical New England conscience which required both sensuous openness to the experience of God's favor and also disciplined adherence to orthodox belief and moral practice. The founders of Massachusetts Bay had been propelled by intense religious emotions, but now, a century later, the repressive influence of moral rigor diminished possibilities. It was easier for new generations to conform than to risk feelings which might not meet the church's expectations. By admitting the children of believers to communion even when they lacked saving experience—a policy pioneered by Edwards' grandfather Solomon Stoddard—Puritans encouraged social conformity while adjusting to the resultant decline in religious emotions. At the same time, however, preachers continued to insist that only heartfelt experience of God's grace would provide the inward assurance that one was not destined for damnation. The Puritan in the pew was in a double bind.

Edwards himself was trained from childhood to regard personal experience of God as the essence of religion, and this conviction was reinforced by his own innovative psychological analysis. Yet the rigor of this same religious training blocked his expressive capacities, and Edwards found that the compromise his grandfather had fashioned was inadequate to resolve the tension he lived with. He kept refining his analysis of religious experience, and perfected his preaching to make the things of God more concrete so his congregation might taste, feel, and know them. He worked for the breakthrough which finally came.

When revival began in Northampton, it met needs deep within Jonathan Edwards. While others were doing the shouting and the weeping, Edwards found his convictions upheld, and this confirmation allowed him to taste more of his own feelings even though he could not express them so publicly. He bent his great talents to encouraging, defending, and understanding the awakening. His writings provided the theological rationale for this new phenomenon.

An irony of the awakening was that the emotional excesses which alarmed so many were actually encouraged by Puritan ecclesiastical paternalism. Eminent ministers defined faith so rigorously and prescribed acceptable experience so carefully that they kept their congregations in childlike dependency. Yet these "children" received a double message: both "behave yourself" and "express yourself." As people felt their power during the emotional heights of awakening, it was natural that—in happy, childish rebellion—they would reach for extremes of expression, enjoying their own release of tension and even enjoying the shock they produced as they exposed the contradiction in the ministers' requirements. Edwards dismissed flamboyant behavior and rebellion against church discipline as secondary characteristics, never realizing that the awakening was inherently disruptive of Puritan order.

Many ministers tried to repress this popular enthusiasm. Some preachers were fully caught up in it and rode the awakening wherever it led them. Edwards, however, never abandoned his analytical responsibilities. He tried desperately to provide guidelines which distinguished godly emotions from misguided enthusiasm, yet he remained trapped by his understanding of his own authority. He was unable to point his parishioners toward an adult faith, unable to tell them "Grow up! Take responsibility for your feelings and your behavior." He could not allow them Christian maturity and restrain himself from continual supervision. The people had to remove him from the pulpit to win this freedom.

Many of Edwards' fellow Puritan and Presbyterian ministers in the American colonies also failed to deal creatively with the psychological consequences of awakening. Among leaders of the Great Awakening in England, however, George Whitefield's gift for arousing feelings was matched by John Wesley's genius for constructing organizations within which the lay people could discipline and channel their own fervor—the "method" which gave Methodism its name. This Methodist marriage of fervor and group discipline would be brought to America in the decades ahead and would evangelize the frontier.[5]

* * *

The Great Awakening began a popular, expressive style of Christianity which we now call "evangelical." It would not have been a large step, within Edwards' psychology, to recognize that nurturing feelings and the expression of affection in the normal flow of human life would help prepare people for a saving meeting with God. However, Edwards did not achieve this insight. John Wesley used the antiquated faculty psychology to affirm "free will" and stress personal choice in saving experience, but he did not recognize that human feeling capacities made their own contribution. The emotional roots of awakening within the human personality were even more mysterious to him than to Edwards.

How different our history might have been if, at this vital beginning, leaders such as Edwards and Wesley could have supported the integrity of human expressiveness. The energetic evangelism of the eighteenth century might have found a point of contact with the political humanism which would shape America's future through that other great awakening, the American Revolution. The political commitment to "life, liberty, and the pursuit of happiness" which inspired a new nation might have found a parallel in a religious commitment to support the full flowering of human life and feeling, so the Lord may be met and served in the world. Such an understanding remains yet to be forged. A fully humane religious culture is yet to be achieved.[6]

*   *   *

While he affirmed that people experience God through their normal psychological capabilities, Edwards also suggested that a saving experience involved a change in personality. Meeting the Lord resulted in a new principle of organization which supported more intense human expression, and in some way the personality was rearranged. Stating this, Edwards acknowledged that he was searching for words, lacking full possession of his insight.

> This new spiritual sense, and the new dispositions that attend it, are no new faculties, but are new principles of nature. I use the word "principles," for want of a word of a more determinate signification. . . . So this new spiritual sense is not a new faculty of understanding, but it is a new foundation laid in the nature of the soul, for a new kind of exercises of the same faculty of understanding. So that new holy disposition of heart that attends this new sense, is not a new faculty of will, but a foundation laid in the nature of the soul, for a new kind of exercise of the same faculty of will.[7]

Meeting the Lord involves a profound discovery of "Who I am." My value in the eyes of God and my place in the world are clarified, and I experience an integrity which releases energy. Knowing who I am, I can live more directly from my desires, in a vital relationship with my environment. To elaborate on what Edwards struggled to express, I have borrowed modern insight on "identity formation" from psychotherapist Erik Erikson. Such a formed identity provides a new foundation for the exercise of all my capabilities.

Identity formation in the presence of God is suggested by the *Shemá*, which summarizes Old Testament faith: "Hear, O Israel, the Lord is our God, one Lord, and you must love the Lord your God with all your heart and soul and strength" (Deuteronomy 6:4,5, NEB). The Lord is distinctively "one," uniquely able to unify human experience. Only if we meet God are we able to make life whole. Only the Lord appropriately calls forth full emotional and intellectual response ("all your heart"), full aliveness (Hebrew *nephesh*, translated "soul"), and full engagement with the world ("strength"). Believing that the "one Lord" is "our God" brings us alive in a unique way. We are known, and therefore we may love.

Writing on the more mundane level of psychological theory, Erik Erikson suggested that forming a sense of personal identity is necessary for a human being to mature into a healthy *psychosocial* organism. That is, I must develop and maintain a clear sense of who I am in relation to the persons, things, ideas, and tasks which form my environment, if I am to live happily and to function effectively. As I achieve insight concerning my identity, I find release of energy for engagement with life. The world and I both benefit as my relationships with my environment become more useful and more satisfying.

Identity formation is often a gradual, unconscious process, but inner tensions and social contradictions may make the process difficult and therefore more apparent. In today's disjointed culture, struggle by adolescents and young adults to fashion identity is often quite visible:

> In some young people, in some classes, at some periods in history, this crisis will be minimal; in other people, classes, and periods, the crisis will be clearly marked off as a critical period, a kind of 'second birth', apt to be aggravated

either by widespread neuroticism or by pervasive ideological unrest. Some young individuals will succumb to this crisis in all manner of neurotic, psychotic, or delinquent behavior; others will resolve it through participation in ideological movements passionately concerned with religion or politics, nature or art. Still others, although suffering and deviating dangerously through what appears to be a prolonged adolescence, eventually come to contribute an original bit to an emerging style of life: the very danger which they have sensed has forced them to mobilize capacities to see and say, to dream and plan, to design and construct, in new ways.[8]

For most of us the discovery and fashioning of identity is not a clean achievement leading smoothly to a useful, happy life. We are too complex, our circumstances too imperfect. Nor do most of us fail so decisively as to be doomed to delinquency and suffering. We carry with us a mixture of achievements and defeats in the formation of a self-understanding related to our environment. This psychosocial process yields both saints and sinners. Through this engagement of self with culture emerge the whole, the maimed, and those with strength enough to continue their struggle.

Erikson's term *identity* highlights a personal sense of "*I*," of awareness. Yet he emphasized that precisely when I know myself, "*I*" am not isolated. I know myself to the degree that I have a coherent relationship with the world around me. "We deal with a process 'located' *in the core of the individual* and yet also *in the core of his communal culture*,"[9] Erikson wrote. Persons and culture influence each other; the culture "molds generations in order to be remolded, to be reinvigorated, by them."[10] Therefore, in this study I call identity an *ecological* reality, since it is realized in relationships. The self-awareness labeled by Erikson as "identity" matches the self-expression that Edwards called "affections" or our earlier definition of *eros* as the continually creative interplay of the full organism with its total environment.

* * *

Erikson hints that identity formation, as he has come to understand it, may depend upon Western culture, even if the process is not experienced as religious. Although he illustrated identity formation with a biographical sketch of George Bernard Shaw, an outspoken atheist,[11] he developed the full complexity of his theory in his major psycho-biographies of religious innovators Martin Luther and Mahatma Gandhi. Since the notions of individuality, identity, and freedom are themselves cultural constructions, Erikson wondered whether the possibility of identity might indeed be rooted in the personality of God at the genesis of our culture.

> How did man's need for individual identity evolve? Before Darwin, the answer was clear: because God created Adam in His own image, as a counterplayer of His Identity, and thus bequeathed to all man[kind] the glory and the despair of individuation and faith. I admit to not having come up with any better explanation.[12]

When he examined religious experience, therefore, Erikson avoided the gratuitous assumption that God is simply a cultural construction. He was aware how complex is the exchange between faith and culture: each influences, and is influenced by, the other. On the other hand, experience of God cannot be isolated from culture. There can be no human experience of God, or of anything else, which does not depend upon one's social setting. Our perceptions are focused and informed by our family and our particular society. We drink deeply of words, images, and cultural expectations in preparation for personal experiences. Without this social help, lone individuals would make little sense of the stimuli flowing toward us from the universe around us. Admitting the importance of culture in this way does not deny "real" experience of a "living" God. Indeed, experience of God may change persons and change culture. It is clear that the image of God in our culture, mediated by the Bible and churches, has profoundly affected our cultural understanding of the world and our self-understanding. Our religious tradition influences the identity even of those who are not consciously religious.

Erikson raised the deep question of whether the psychosocial construction he called "identity" was not itself dependent upon this distinctive religious tradition. As centuries of interaction with the biblical Lord have shaped our culture, specific expectations for human nature have developed, one of which is the expectation that persons can interact with the world creatively, responsibly, and with meaning. This expectation has been reinforced by those who have lived in faith. The cultural possibility of fashioning a psychosocial identity may depend, at least in part, upon this religious tradition.

16. *Moral Beauty*

Experience of the Lord forms identity: this capacity distinguishes the biblical Lord from idols who receive our projections but cannot interact. Far from violating our psychological unity, God helps us to achieve integrity. One person's religious experience, therefore, may not duplicate another's; it may not conform to a pattern or be limited by boundaries suggested in the Christian tradition. Although the Lord is a distinct personality, part of God's personality is reticence. God does not disclose fully. God's face remains hidden:

> Truly, thou art a God who hidest thyself,
> O God of Israel, the Savior. (Isaiah 45:15, RSV)

Jesus was reluctant to identify himself in a way that would close his hearers' search for understanding. Though it may make us anxious, God's reticence stimulates us to discover ourselves within our faith. Beauty can emerge from God's hiding.[1]

Each person may see God from a different vantage and each age may present the Lord in a different light. Personal experience sharpens the generalized image of God presented by a culture. As a consequence of many such experiences, along with other historical events, social understanding of the Lord's personality changes and grows. In this way the cultural image of God remains relevant and challenging.

I have argued that beauty is manifest when beings support the life and individuality of each other. Moral beauty is the conscious choice to do so.[2] I now turn to the kernel of Edwards' religious insight: *a person is made whole through sensuous awakening to the beauty of the Lord.* Edwards himself put it this way:

The first effect of the power of God in the heart in REGEN-
ERATION is to give the heart a Divine taste of sense; to
cause it to have a relish of the loveliness and sweetness of
the supreme excellency of the Divine nature; and indeed
this is all the immediate effect of the Divine Power that
there is, this is all the Spirit of God needs to do, in order to
a production of all good effects in the soul.[3]

I find this a striking insight into Christian experience. All
gracious benefits to human character flow naturally from this
new taste. To account for new life in a Christian, we need not
imagine, as some theologies suggest, divine manipulation of
the human personality.

I have chosen the word *sensuous* to convey what I
believe Edwards meant by his awkward phrase "taste of
sense," and also by his more expressive phrase "relish of the
loveliness and sweetness."[4] Edwards' reference includes what
we might identify as sensory, emotional, and intuitive capacities. Each of these aspects of the personality—indeed the
whole personality—is involved in experience of God. Edwards
emphasized that experience of God's beauty has a striking
sensuous quality. It is a "tasting" experience—an immediate,
inward sense which is only possible when fear is overcome;[5] it
engages the emotions, stimulates intuition, and heightens the
senses. From such experience, human renewal emerges re-
sponsively. Without such experience, God remains a cultural
image lacking vital impact.

I have suggested that God's beauty, manifest in the
act of beautifying, emerges in creativity. God's distinctive creative expression is fashioning other life, each with its own
center, its own individuality. Then, in Edwards' words, "God
delights in communicating his happiness to the creature."[6]

Edwards believed that the experience of God's *moral
beauty* elicits human awakening. He also called this the
"beauty of holiness," as when he stated "A love to divine
things for the beauty and sweetness of their moral excellency,
is the first beginning and spring of all holy affections. . . . The
beauty of holiness . . . is the quality that is the immediate

object" of human awareness in experience of the Lord. For example, Edwards suggested, it is when we sense "the beauty of the moral perfection of Christ" that we can accept Jesus as mediator, reconciling us to God.[7]

Experience of God's beauty is far more, however, than awareness of perfection in another. The taste for moral beauty comes with the gift of relationship. Psalm 18 (NEB, alt.) expresses how David's faith was grounded in his experience of God's favor and delight.

> [God] brought me out into an open place,
> [God] rescued me because God delighted in me. (vs. 19)

This confidence filled him with energy: "With thy help I leap over a bank, by God's aid I spring over a wall" (vs.29), but it also aroused moral commitment. Ethics spring to life when we are in God's presence, aware of God's love:

> I have followed the ways of the Lord
> and have not turned wickedly from my God;
> all [God's] laws are before my eyes . . . (vss. 21–22)

David conveyed his sense of God's presence through poetic stanzas about storms, earthquakes, and political upheavals. The presence was real, but God remained veiled by thick darkness.

> [The Lord] made darkness . . . a hiding-place
> and dense vapour [a] canopy. (vs. 11)

This veiling, this divine reticence, was an important and gracious part of God's presence. It allowed David to find himself.

> Thou hast given me the shield of thy salvation,
> thy hand sustains me, thy [humility] makes me great.
> Thou givest me room for my steps,
> my feet have not faltered. (vss. 35–36)[8]

God's moral beauty is this distinctive gift of loving, challenging presence that yet allows the other "room for my steps."

* * *

Moral beauty appeals to us. It distinguishes the Lord

from many other gods who have occupied human attention. Gods often objectify power, drawing their apparent vitality from human anxiety and fear; a moral relationship, however, is built on reassurance. *Moral* suggests that the quality of the relationship has implications for the life and conduct of both parties. It is not simply that God is "loving" or "just": these abstractions fall short. The Lord's love and justice are qualities stimulated within relationship. They are covenant characteristics, expressing not just divine attributes, but divine bonding and commitment. Therefore Hebrews could imagine that at the beginnings of their tribal relationship with the Lord, Jacob wrestled with God for a blessing, and Abraham bargained with God to limit the Lord's righteous fury.[9] Relationships are formed through real interchange.

We have human experience of love deepening through time, even in a difficult relationship. This prepares us to appreciate how God, after long history, was ready to express love for the world so fully in the sacrifice of Christ. The gift of Jesus emerged from God's engagement with the world, and because of Jesus the potential for human response to God enlarged.

Recognizing God's moral beauty stimulates insight about one's role, duties, and opportunities. Moral experience is more than awe and submission before a mighty God, though these elements are often present. Experience of the Lord is ecological (or as Erikson would call it, cultural); it brings to light whole networks of God's relationships with the earth. Ethical content is at its core. Persons may emerge from this experience with new convictions, a new sense of truth. They are likely to feel affirmed, forgiven, emboldened. They may see more clearly their work and their opportunities to engage with the world. Also, they are quite likely to feel moral obligation: insight, energy, and commitment in relation to some object which has now become their special concern. Biblically, this last is the most characteristic consequence of meeting God. Most of those whose experiences are remembered in Scripture do not linger in the temple. They know themselves called to "follow me," to "lead my people out," to "speak my word," or to "feed my sheep."

Beauty expresses the attractiveness of this moral relationship. Experience of God is exciting when it yields the profound "Aha!" of insight and releases emotional energy for living. There is deep satisfaction in identity formation as Erikson described it, coming to know oneself as welcomed and useful in a meaningful world, but experience of the Lord adds another aspect to this. At the core of my own experience I taste another Personality, whose integrity and concern stretch my capacity to imagine. I discover my identity in the presence of Another. This relationship continues as I live and work, when I fail, and when I grow and change. Over time I glimpse new aspects of the Lord who challenges me to new growth and fresh commitments. Through times of revelation and times of hiding, the relationship continues, a "blessed assurance." It is beautiful.

The beauty of the Lord is personal. God's love and goodness, God's righteousness and power, God's mystery and elusiveness, are all facets of God's character. God's beauty has profound metaphysical, theological, and ethical implications. But this God cannot be reduced to abstractions, states of being, theological formulas, or rules for life. We meet God as a personality. We meet "Yahweh" in the Old Testament (whose Hebrew name I render "Lord" in these pages, following common English usage). We meet Jesus. Christians affirm that in meeting this personality we know God most clearly. In Jesus' equation, "I am the truth" (John 14:6, KJV), the "I" dominates, for the "I" is the more revealing word. Truth derives from a relationship.

Because its focus is personality, experience of God is not reserved for the sophisticated. Edwards reminded us that it is a concrete, "sensible" experience, available to "men of mean capacities."[10] Some people may merely experience "Jesus loves me, this I know," and from the beauty of this realization they emerge renewed.

* * *

There are many stories and sayings in the Bible which do not express moral beauty to me, but each story and saying has been part of someone's experience with the Lord. At some time or another, each has been beautiful: to the one who lived the event or received the insight, to those who told the tale, or to those who heard and remembered the words. The beauty of the Lord appears in this specific, relevant connection to persons in different situations. God does not remain abstracted; the Lord does not value consistency above relevance. God reaches to people where we are, and speaks to us in the context of our culture and understanding.

For forty years I have been reading the Bible. I am often surprised when words, read before and almost unnoticed, now address me with fresh meaning. On the other hand, markings in my Bibles also remind me of the passages I have found nourishing before, some of which are less interesting now, and a few even troublesome or offensive, for I have changed, and times have changed. The Lord I met in Scripture has probed me, challenged me to grow, stimulated my changes, and tolerated my incompleteness. I find this beautiful.

Another person may respond to different biblical images or draw different insights from texts which I also treasure. We may argue and I may be amazed that someone could draw such strange ideas from his or her relationships with God. My doubt is probably misplaced, for I do not possess the Lord, who remains free to relate to others in ways I cannot follow.

In this generation, God is hidden from many. As my environmental concerns join me with people outside church organizations, I sometimes glimpse the beauty of God in hiding. One friend may have such different life experiences that none of my religious culture has meaning to him or her. To this person the name of the Lord means nothing; it may even be offensive. Yet this friend also lives with integrity. We join together in tasks which I see as a response to God's calling and a witness to God's justice, although this friend may not understand the religious meaning which I attach to our shared work. I thank the Lord for sustaining a world where those who do not knowingly experience God may also work for the integrity of life. In this I see God's moral beauty.

The living God is a relevant Lord. No other god is so beautiful.

17. *Wholeness*

Erik Erikson recognized that religion is often important to the healthy development of personal identity, development which manifests "wholeness." Sometimes, however, he saw religion contribute to an identity disturbance in which a person clings to "totalisms."

Wholeness, to Erikson, means organic flexibility. One's sense of identity, like other parts of a healthy organism, is responsive. It may be bent under frustration and yet return to shape with reassurance. One may become anxious or confused and yet recover. A person with a whole identity has capacity to grow. Erikson suggests that the "boundaries" between a healthy personality and the surrounding culture, part of self-definition, are nevertheless "open and fluid."[1] Judgments concerning the world may change with experience and insight. Such healthy growth stimulates creative adaptation under changing circumstances. In Erikson's theory this wholeness depends, in turn, upon basic trust in life—confidence that there can be fruitful interaction between a person and his or her environment. Basic trust is formed in infancy with help from nurturing parents.

Totalisms, on the other hand, are rigid commitments which manifest distrust of the larger world. The word derives from Erikson's analysis of the psychology of totalitariansim. When a sense of personhood is based on totalisms, identification with a race, a group, or an idea is complete, yet it is anxious. The person guards against polluting contact with those who are different: "An absolute boundary is emphasized: . . . nothing that belongs inside must be left outside, nothing that must be outside can be tolerated inside."[2] The person has a defensive rigidity that prevents growth by inhibiting new relationships and new experiences. Many young adults exhibit clearly one of these contrasting identities. One person may appear purposeful, yet poised and confident. Another is intense, anxious, and argumentative, with a ready but shallow smile which holds people at a distance.

In Western society, Erikson observes, religion is the cultural institution that supports the basic trust we learned as infants from parental care. This fundamental trust in life makes wholeness possible. Religion helps a person experience this trust in subsequent stages of life. Religious experience can also help repair trust that has been damaged by adversity, and it can even help a person build trust when infantile experience was inadequate.

> In the establishment of psychosocial identity ... an ideological formula, intelligible both in terms of individual development and of significant tradition, must do for the young person what the mother did for the infant: provide nutriment for the soul as well as for the stomach, and screen the environment so that vigorous growth may meet what it can manage.
> Of all the ideological systems, however, only religion restores the earliest sense of appeal to a Provider, a Providence. In the Judaeo-Christian tradition, no prayer indicates this more clearly than "The Lord make His Face to shine upon you and be gracious unto you. The Lord lift up His countenance upon you and give you peace."[3]

When trust breaks down, when a person despairs of finding an embracing relationship with the world, immersion in totalisms can provide a feeling of safety. Although totalisms are particularly tempting during the anxious adolescent years when one is searching for identity, they may also appeal at other times when one's sense of identity is fragile. Erikson believes it may be normal to revert to totalisms in a period of acute stress. When the emergency passes, a healthy person can resynthesize a more flexible identity. Some persons, however, remain prisoners of rigidity.

During times of social crisis when many persons feel

threatened, totalitarian leaders exploit the people's fear. They propose simplistic answers to complex problems; invite persons to join rigid cults, disciplined armies, or intense conspiracies; and cultivate rage against those outside their group whom they portray as threatening. Erikson suggested that the power of such leaders comes from their ability to release the deep rage of those they influence, directing it against objects of the leader's choosing.[4] This rage goes beyond conscious, appropriate anger at particular circumstances. In Erikson's psychoanalytic perspective, such rage draws from a deposit of resentments trapped within those subjected to cruelty or exploitation in childhood. This deep rage is often both blind and blinding when it emerges.

> The polarity adult-child is the first in the inventory of existential oppositions (male-female being the second) which makes man exploitable and induces him to exploit. The child's inborn proclivity for feeling powerless, deserted, ashamed, and guilty in relation to those on whom he depends is systematically utilized for his training, often to the point of exploitation . . . with the result that impotent rage is stored up where energy should be free for productive development.[5]

Totalitarian leaders draw their satisfaction from the exercise of power. The potential scope of their power is enhanced by modern communications and sophisticated organizational techniques. Other leaders, not consciously totalitarian, may exploit anger to divert attention from their failure to resolve real problems. Totalisms can be cultivated to bolster nationalism or racism, to support churches or political parties. They are not life-giving, since they enslave people to their fears. Some totalisms may exploit the symbols of Christianity, but they do not represent the will of God.

Christians may profitably reflect on Erikson's distinction between wholeness and totalisms. Biblical religion has nurtured our trust that life is in the hands of God, that the world is meaningful, and that persons can engage purposefully with the environment which God created and sustains. Biblical religion and "Christian culture" have been distinctive supports for the formation of identity as Erikson portrays it. Sometimes, however, Christian leaders and church groups have used totalitarian techniques to induce narrow, rigid commitment that does not give life.

When Jonathan Edwards preached "Sinners in the Hands of an Angry God," he was brainwashing. Using psychological understanding new to his day, and devising innovative techniques of oratory, he projected images which overwhelmed the imagination of his hearers.[6] Adolf Hitler would perfect similar oratorical techniques, and combine them with theatrical devices, to overwhelm his German audiences in the 1930s. Lacking a psychology of the unconscious, Edwards could not know that he tapped buried feelings unrelated to his religious objective. He did observe that many feelings awakened among his hearers had little to do with experience of God's beauty, but he did not associate this result with the character of the stimulus he provided.

Today's preachers cannot afford to be ignorant of human psychology or to ignore relationships between faith and health. If we appreciate Erikson's useful distinction between *wholeness* and *totalisms*, we can review our own use of words and images to see whether they truly help people experience God's beauty and fashion a deep, flexible, and creative faith. Since we are properly anxious about the spread of tyrannies in the world, we can eschew religious approaches that repress feelings, exploit fear or anger, or encourage moral dependency. When we fail to help people toward freedom, faith, and wholeness, they remain vulnerable to exploitation by deliberate tyrants.

It is important for all Christians to trust God enough to step free from our anxious rigidities, acknowledge our own feelings, and allow ourselves to grow. These steps will lead, I believe, toward deeper experience of the Lord. Then we can tolerate and support others who also claim such freedom.

18. *A Relevant Lord*

A person is made whole through sensuous awakening to the beauty of the Lord. This is the heart of the matter, for Jonathan Edwards and in my own thinking as well. I return to my inference from this understanding of beauty because it has important practical consequences. *The beauty of the Lord undergirds the existence of God.* Beauty comes first; we begin with an appreciation of God's character before we deal with the question of God's existence. Rational speculation, prior to experience, is likely to be stale and unprofitable.

This insight tempers the impact of relativism on faith. "Relativism" is the theory that truth is relative to the individual and to the time and place within which the individual acts. An inference from this perspective is that no absolute truth stands authoritatively above us to guide human behavior. Once we acknowledge that perceptions of God and conclusions of religion are conditioned by time, place, and culture, the relativist perspective may be used to suggest, "Really, there is no God."[1]

Edwards said that God is distinguished chiefly by divine beauty.[2] He came to this insight in response to the challenge of conflicting interpretations of faith. Edwards had not wished to disrupt the religious monopoly which his ancestors came to Massachusetts to secure, but the Great Awakening had released new energies which the cautiously orthodox found irregular and dangerous. On the other hand, some preachers of the awakening accused their critics of lacking essential Christian experience, and therefore knowing nothing of true faith. Edwards tried to dig deeper than the competing claims of the fervid and the orthodox. Concluding that the core of true religion was experience of the beauty of the Lord, he was confident that those who shared such experience would feel deeply, that they could usually be led to correct doctrine, and that they would generally live in a way appropriate to Christians. But neither deep feelings as such, nor the profession of doctrine, nor the practice of piety was the font of saving faith. Saving faith was simply knowing the beauty of the Lord.

Within this biblical tradition of moral beauty, I see how we may avoid both the rigidity of absolutism and the despair of relativism. The Lord of biblical experience engages life and history relevantly. This Lord sought out Moses, training him to words and deeds that liberated a people and forged a purposeful community. Through prophets, God spoke with these chosen people. In a full range of historical situations, the Hebrews engaged one Lord, yet found God's word relevant. Christians have trusted that God's most complete revelation is not a set of eternal principles, but a particular life lived in one time and place. "And the Word became flesh and dwelt among us, full of grace and truth; we have beheld his glory" (John 1:14, RSV). The beauty of God was revealed clearly in the personality, words, and deeds of Jesus.

Secular historians of culture would agree that the biblical deity has survived as a potent image in cultural history because this God has been adapted so creatively to changing circumstances. Through constant reinterpretation of words and images, some of which advance into consciousness while others recede, a complex fabric of moral meaning has continued to influence our culture. Throughout Western history people have responded to this tradition. Some have experienced the Lord, and they have changed. Even when institutions claiming to represent God have been oppressive, prophets informed by this moral tradition have arisen to proclaim liberation in the name of the Lord.

If, by the "beauty of the Lord," we mean no more than the moral and psychic relevance of this complex mythology,

then from a simply historical point of view the continued
vitality of this God in culture has been a confirmation of
beauty. Historically, the being of God has depended upon the
beauty of God. Had the mythology not remained vital and
relevant to different times and circumstances, other deities
and values would have replaced the Lord. There are always
competitors.

Both philosophical and scientific patterns of thought
challenge this biblical tradition of moral beauty. Philosophical modes of thinking, which the Greeks contributed to
Western culture, tempt us to define God as a fixed being with
consistent attributes that make sense within this particular
system of language. Philosophical analysis may serve not to
expand our understanding of God, but to constrict it.
Philosophical language leads people to think of God as abstract, fixed, and unresponsive. Such a perspective can
inhibit the relationship at the heart of biblical faith.

The habits of thought and systems of language used
by natural science create similar problems. Natural science
tends to confine reality to things known without feeling,
things perceived by objective tools of measurement. This perspective cannot embrace experience of the beauty of the Lord
which is at the heart of biblical faith, because it eliminates
what Edwards called "sensible knowledge"—knowledge involving the full sensuous personality.

I do not suggest isolating experience of God from rational reflection or scientific inquiry. Since the experience of God's
beauty stimulates awareness of meaningful relationship with
the world, which is the context of life, we would violate the character of this experience by sheltering it. Exploring links between
religious faith and other knowledge is always appropriate, for
religious conviction should be open to criticism from other perspectives. One will enhance the moral relevance of faith if one
holds this experience open to everything in life. Faith grounded
in moral beauty does not need anxious protection.

Such wholeness is not likely to collapse under challenge. A believer may be confronted occasionally with an

intellectual critique to which he or she does not have a ready response. At another time the believer may know strong, new feelings, or may face moral decisions for which he or she feels inadequate. Such challenges make a person want to seek the Lord again, open to growing insight. Sometimes there is a long wait, with pain and struggle, until a new sense of moral coherence becomes clear. This sense may include new understanding of God and fresh self-understanding. When faith is alive and growing, hope, courage, and enthusiasm for life can also be renewed. Our relationship with the Lord can be relevant, not rigid. This is the beauty of the Lord.

* * *

I believe the Lord is more than a cultural artifact, more than a magnificent image cast up in human history, refined and elaborated by generations of moral creativity— though a God no more than that might still be worthy of commitment. Cultural constructions can be beautiful, and many are essential to human life. Some human constructions such as the American Constitution and particularly the Bill of Rights, I would risk my life to protect. If the Lord were a moral reality of this type, the Lord might still be worth living for, even dying for.

Yet I know the Lord as more than this. Edwards has helped me account for this knowledge, since he wrestled with a similar concern. True, he did not deal with skeptics who denied the existence of God. In Puritan New England no one denied God's existence, not publicly at least. The Awakening, however, fostered a parallel concern. Edwards wanted to distinguish those who passively accepted the cultural myth from those who, indeed, knew God. The Puritan monopoly within New England made it easy to coast through life with an unthinking acceptance of familiar doctrine and a habitual adherence to approved behavior. To Edwards this had no more value than skepticism. It was indeed more subversive of true faith than skepticism, because it required no emotional awareness, no reflection, no perception, no decision. Passive belief left persons unfinished, less than alive.

Puritans felt that the "saints," those who knew God, must be different from passive followers. Edwards tried to focus upon "that idea which the saint has of the loveliness of God, and that sensation, and that kind of delight he has in that view"—the phenomenon which distinguishes a relationship with the living God.[3] His conclusion was that the real believer falls in love with the beauty of the Lord.

> The first foundation of a true love to God, is that whereby he is in himself lovely, or worthy to be loved, or the supreme loveliness of his nature. . . . How can that be true love of beauty and brightness, which is not for beauty and brightness' sake?[4]

Today we know that the beginnings of love often include projection, a state in which unacknowledged feelings within oneself are imagined as coming from the beloved. The lover eagerly anticipates what the beloved may return. After all, love is not disinterested; the lover hopes to be nourished in body and soul. Mutual love, however, creates a relationship within which each partner can learn to honor the other. Each can learn how to meet his or her own needs, how to nourish the other, and how to support the integrity of the relationship itself. Love is fulfilled when two people grow beyond their projections and self-interests. As they begin truly to see, know, and care for each other, their giving and receiving express beauty of love.

My own relationship with God began with acute consciousness of need, as well as many projections about the character of this God who responded to me. But as the contact continued and deepened, I became more fascinated with the beauty of the Lord. It was this Lord who reached out to me, freely giving, to create the relationship. The tales of this Lord revealed an intricate connection with the world, articulated through acts of compassion and demands for justice. My relationship was informed by what I understood about the Lord from the religious tradition, yet nevertheless it remains my unique relationship. As experience with God grows, my desire expands beyond the wish to be saved, to focus on serving and knowing the Lord. The relationship becomes a real meeting of two personalities.

Thus I know the Lord the way I know another person. Although my culture has taught me what to notice in persons and how to engage with them, when I really get to know a person, I move beyond etiquette and accepted standards of evaluation. I acquire what Edwards called "sensible knowledge," rooted in my own senses, feelings, and experience. Just so, I know the Lord through intuitive inferences I now trust. In his quaint style Edwards said the same thing:

> This view or sense of the divine glory, and unparalleled beauty of the things exhibited to us in the gospel, has a tendency to convince the mind of their divinity. . . . He that truly sees the divine, transcendent, supreme glory of those things which are divine, does as it were know their divinity intuitively.[5]

Some have called this intuition a "leap of faith." But the leap actually follows the intuition: it is a leap *from* faith. The leap is not one of imagination, reaching out to conjure up an image of God; it is better not to make such a leap. Nor is the leap a decision to accept the authority of some person, institution, or Scripture, for if that requires a leap, the decision is not an appropriate one. Wait for experience of the beauty of the Lord. Wait for moving insight which makes sense of your life in God's presence. Then leap. The leap is a willingness to trust what you know—a willingness to live.

Part V.

Nature

I went to the Garden of Love.
And saw what I never had seen:
A Chapel was built in the midst,
Where I used to play on the green.

And the gates of this Chapel were shut,
And Thou shalt not, writ over the door;
So I turn'd to the Garden of Love,
That so many sweet flowers bore,

And I saw it was filled with graves,
And tomb-stones where flowers should be:
And Priests in black gowns, were walking their rounds,
And binding with briars, my joys & desires.

William Blake
Songs of Experience, 1794[1]

I am pained by Blake's words because I cannot avoid their truth. Modern Christianity has often bound our "joys and desires," and the church has also, sometimes, viewed nature as a competitor. Through indifference, it has tolerated modern society's war against nature. I believe this need not be true. Faith in the biblical Lord is more properly expressive than repressive, and Christian identity rightly includes respect for life, affection for nature, and concern for all God's creation. The church may join nature in the sabbath of praise; it need not compete with nature for our Lord's attention.

Isolation from sensuous contact with living things, and with the forces and materials of the natural world, damages the human personality. Christian identity, in particular, is incomplete if it does not embrace moral experience with nature. Yet urban, technological culture threatens men and women with such isolation. Christians can respond to this threat if we see the relation between Christ and nature from a new perspective. The world in which God delights is being damaged by human oppression, and Christ is the suffering servant sharing the pain of the "least of these." When we care for natural life that God loves, we truly meet Christ.

Humanity has a vocation to enrich the biosphere by adding awareness, creativity, and protection. Our knowledge can help the earth to know itself. Like our Lord, we can choose to confer beauty rather than to oppress nature, and furthermore, we can affirm our terrestrial destiny. When we appreciate our place in an ecosystem where death contributes to new life, death itself may acquire new meaning for us.

19. *Nature in Human Identity*

For the first time in history, we have developed in the West a society where the majority of men and women do not live and work in direct contact with the land, the sea, or the species of natural life. We are becoming an urban culture. Even in "underdeveloped" countries there is a strong trend in this direction. Our food is processed and packaged. In our daily work most of us do not shape organic materials using skills responsive to natural properties. We do not weave flax or work in wood. Where we do use such materials, we feed them into machines after growing the varieties that fit the requirements of these machines. Our work relates predominantly to the tools of culture, not to the materials of nature.

We are becoming more *humanocentric:* nearly everything that forms our sense of self, our feeling of place, and our experience of culture is a human construction. We have pets, and we use living plants for landscaping and decoration, but we need not engage with nature seriously. When we choose to meet nature, it is usually for recreation.

Fewer people till the land, cut the forests, mine the minerals, or fish the seas. But the earth does not benefit from this reduced human presence; indeed, we burden the earth even more than before. We lumber, farm, mine, and fish with bigger machines and more potent chemicals. Those who engage with the earth are trained not to live with nature, but simply to harvest from it. Agriculture, which once involved complex traditions of working in productive harmony with land, has been replaced by "agribusiness," the single-minded exploitation of the earth for profit. As society leaves the earth to machines, and the remaining few who live with nature are trained to think like machines, the earth suffers.

Hunters once had a keen appreciation of the wisdom and skills of their prey; they also respected the predatory animals who competed with them. Those who worked with domestic animals or rode horses into battle developed complex, intuitive communication between person and beast. Those who grew crops, tended vines, or shaped trees became sensitive to the vitality of the plants they knew well and the environment they tended with care. Few of us now have these opportunities.

The human species evolved in natural settings and was shaped through interplay with other forms of life. We share sensory abilities and physiological characteristics with a variety of other living creatures. Each species has particular skills, some more developed than our own, that have evolved along with their ecological niche. Many species have mental and emotional capacities that are more sensitive and sophisticated than science is ready to acknowledge. With bias toward human control of other life, scientists tend to ignore evidence of those traits in other species which might suggest we have ethical obligations toward them.[1]

Humans once functioned in complex natural ecosystems, attuned to their fruitfulness. Modern culture, however, has surrendered those skills for riskier strategies of control. Genetic researcher Wes Jackson describes an ecosystem as a complex of information developed over vast periods of time and stored, not in brains or computers, but in the genes and interrelationships of thousands of species. Natural environments are generally far more complex and dense with life than the civilized constructions that have replaced them, whether these be farms or shopping malls. Though we may sometimes enrich a landscape, most often human dominion simplifies nature so it can be controlled. We replace complex ecosystems with vast fields of one crop where unwanted life is suppressed. To maintain control we hold more information in our minds and in cultural repositories. Still, total environmental information may be depleted. The new system, producing what humans desire, is not as sophisticated as the self-regulating ecosystem it replaced. It is more vulnerable to weather and blight. It requires more nourishment from outside the system, and constant supervision. Jackson concludes that despite centuries of human dominion, "less cultural information is present on the earth than is biological information. To destroy biological information and expect cultural information to take its place on a one-to-one basis is risky."[2]

The human species pays a high price for the benefits we receive. Although we have developed techniques to produce more of what we wish to consume, we are losing the ability to relate to life, to listen to other species, to cooperate with the earth. We are becoming aliens in our homeland. Ironically, we must now devote an increasing proportion of our work and resources to protecting ourselves from the undesired consequences of human administration of the earth. As deforestation dries ecosystems, for example, we pipe our water from greater distances and clean it to remove filth from our own society. We spin in vicious circles. Cities exhaust heat and air pollutants, forcing us to air-condition buildings so we may breathe safely and work in comfort; in turn, the energy required for air-conditioning further pollutes the air and raises temperatures. Sometimes—as when agricultural mechanization drives people from the land to urban slums—our narrowly purposeful manipulation of nature creates environments alien to both natural life and human culture.

Modern men and women are so thoroughly surrounded by constructions of human culture that they may become imprisoned, walled off from the world beyond. I recognize that culture, humanity's crowning achievement, is essential to us. The human species is now a cultural construction, as well as a biological one. The rich human capacities to sense, to understand, to feel and to express all depend upon cultural institutions and images that symbolize and stimulate these capacities. Culture at its best relates humans to themselves, to other persons, to their history and potential, and to the natural world within which human life is set. Yet when personal contacts with the world beyond the human begin to shrivel, people lose a sense of reality. Awareness of God and communion with nature diminish as people are isolated by the press of other people and by society's products, ideas, and institutions. In the late 1960s some people proclaimed that "God is dead," while others discovered that "Nature is dying." The sense of God's death reflects the anxiety created by the modern myth that nothing is meaningful beyond human culture. Our parallel fear for the death of nature grows from our discovery that human dominion has consequences we do not foresee and cannot control. The first victim of the modern age, however, is a human culture turned in upon itself and weakened by its own introversion.

We have seen that human identity, our sense of who we are, is a functional, meaningful relationship between the inner "I" and the outer world which we see as context for our life. This is a world of people and things, of history, values, and expectations. Until recently it has usually been a world with a specific landscape and many living creatures besides humans. It is not the presence of nature as scenery which makes nature valuable for our identity but interactions which provide material support, stimulate our senses, stretch our intuition, elicit our moral regard, and challenge our creativity. One finds meaning as a farmer, another as a woodworker, another as a resident of a landscape that has become a community of friends. Each of these people has experiences and relationships that give perspective on the claims of human culture. Relationships beyond culture protect our freedom from social control.

Isolation from both God and nature increases our vulnerability to oppression from within society. Culture, like a looking glass, focuses, magnifies, and tints all human experience. One danger is that a few may come to control the shape of what we see. If a substantial part of human experience derives from realities in our environment beyond human control—if we know God and work with nature—we have resources to resist brainwashing through popular images.

Although the maturing of human dominion on earth has threatening potential, it also presents opportunities for fresh perspectives on nature. Historically, attitudes toward nature have been tinged with fear derived from society's vulnerability to the powers of nature. Now we are more secure. We do not fear nature; we fear *for* nature. Human attitudes were once colored, as we have seen, by necessary but uncomfortable intimacy with other creatures. Now our problem is structured isolation from other life. Once the peasant stood anxiously at the rough meeting of human skill with natural forces, while those in manor house or town dwelt with more peace of mind. Now anxiety is the urban disease which we assuage by reaching out to landscapes that provide relief from society. For the first time in human history it is necessary for most of us to consciously affirm and actively pursue natural relationships that previous generations took for granted.

The rhythms of human communication are rapid; we learn from one another quickly. We must often change rhythms when we attend to other life which communicates with slower cycles. Learning from nature may require attention spans of an hour, a season, or perhaps a lifetime. The forms of nature's communication differ as well from the language and cultural imagery with which we are familiar, so that listening stretches our senses, our imagination, and our intuition. This is what makes tending a garden, fishing a stream, and hiking a wilderness refreshing; they call forth perceptive, emotional, and intuitive skills not well used in social relationships. They exercise psychic muscles which have shrunk. They open new worlds. "Man is but the place where I stand," Thoreau said, "and the prospect hence is infinite. It is not a chamber of mirrors which reflect me."[3]

To find ourselves as humans, to emerge from modern society's gilded hall of mirrors, men and women need to engage deliberately with nature. Aldo Leopold said that professionals who guide people to nature should have one goal in mind: "To promote perception is the only truly creative part of recreational engineering."[4] Poet Gary Snyder knows that we must attune to nature's longer rhythms to hear her deepest notes. To help children grow in communion with nature, he advises, we will need to design experiences once common within a rooted culture.

> By our grandchildren's time there may begin to be a culture of place again in America. How does this work? First, a child must experience that bonding to place that has always touched many of us deeply: a small personal territory one can run to, a secret "fort," a place of never-forgotten smells and sounds, a refuge away from home. Second, one must continue to live in a place, to not move away, and to continue walking the paths and roads. A child's walking the land is a veritable exercise in "expanding consciousness." Third, one must have human teachers, who can name and explain the plants, who know the life cycle of an area. Fourth, one must draw some little part of one's livelihood from the breadth of the landscape: spotting downed trees for next year's firewood, gathering mushrooms or berries or herbs on time, fishing, hunting, scrounging. Fifth, one must learn to listen. Then the voice can be heard. The nature spirits are never dead, they are alive under our feet, over our heads, all around us, ready to speak when we are silent and centered. So what is this "voice"? Just the cry of a flicker, or coyote, or jay, or wind in a tree, or acorn whack on a garage roof. Nothing mysterious, but now you're home.[5]

Reincorporating nature into human identity presents a special challenge to Christians. Christian identity takes many forms, relevant to the needs of the "I" met by God in a particular culture and environment. At its most desperate, it is the identity of life's prisoner who finds solace in no one and no thing, but like Job cries out to the Lord in agony and expectation and receives, if not an explanation, at least God's presence. This identity has no positive social or environmental content, but it is a cry for release from this world to something better. Since in our age there remain many who are tortured and abused, God will continue to meet men and women in this way.

More blessed is the one who, however difficult the situation, shares it with friends who accept their lot together. Here, meeting God involves discovering love for my neighbor as well. Through loving my sister and brother whom I see, I make tangible my love for the Lord who remains beyond sight.[6] At this stage Christian identity embraces God and fellow believers, making a church possible. If the rest of the world is perceived as hostile and threatening, this fellowship may be a narrow sect with high walls, a group bound by totalisms, a band hoping to survive this world while awaiting the next.

As believers gain confidence and strength, however, God challenges us to move outward, and expand our community: to regard the slave as well as the free, the Greek as well as Jew. Then, as we are able to respond, God calls us to open ourselves to those in the world with whom we do not share commitment. "I say to you, Love your enemies and pray for those who persecute you, so that you may be [children of God who] . . . makes [the] sun rise on the evil and on the good, and sends rain on the just and on the unjust" (Matthew 5:44–45, RSV, alt.). Mature Christian identity includes deep, caring relationships that permeate this world, in the image of God who loved the world so much as to send Jesus.[7] It becomes our vocation to engage with the life around us.

Christians have often regarded nature as an enemy or treated it as a slave. This is now a dangerous immaturity. Paul says, "The creation waits with eager longing for the revealing of the [children] of God" (Romans 8:19, RSV, alt.). The time is at hand to break down this dividing wall that separates us from our natural environment so we may complete the fellowship of faith.

20. *Christ in Nature*

From the time that young Jonathan built "a booth in a swamp, in a very retired spot," communion with nature played a vital role in Edwards' expressive life.[1] In such retirement he found relief from the pressures of a large, ministerial household—first his father's, later his own. Protected by this seclusion the child learned to explore his environment with his own senses, producing essays such as "Of Insects" and "Of the Rainbow," which showed remarkable gifts of observation and analysis. Later, following the Northampton revival, when Edwards was eager to complete his own conversion and give expression to his deepest yearnings, he went again "into the woods . . . in a retired place," where he had his most profound experience of the presence and love of Christ.[2]

For those who are shy in human company, as Edwards was, experience with nature can be especially important. Here the mysterious constraints learned in childhood, which inhibit free expression in the presence of other persons, may not apply. In the woods Edwards did not have to feel responsible for his surroundings. He could take in sights, sounds, and sensations without screening them. He could respond with expressions of gratitude and joy, with tears and songs, more exuberantly than in the presence of his congregation or even his family.

This impression is confirmed by a remarkable comment in a brief private essay Edwards wrote on "The Beauty of the World." Most of the essay is speculation about form, color, and the place of human consent in the psychology of perception. But in a final appended note, Edwards' feelings break through. "Corollary: Hence the reason why almost all men, and those that seem to be very miserable, love life, because they cannot bear to lose sight of such a beautiful and lovely world." Even though we may not dwell on this beauty every day, he continued, it brings the type of pleasure that, "when we come to the trial, we had rather live in much pain and misery than lose."[3]

We would not expect Edwards, like some modern biological theorists, to consider human beings' will to live merely the result of a genetically programmed urge to survive. His psychology was relational: motivations for life come from the sensuous quality of relationships with others. But it is striking that here Edwards ascribed the motivation for life to the beauty of contact with nature, rather than to joys found in human companionship. Whether or not it is true for most people that the beauty of nature heals despair and provides motivation for living, it apparently was true for Edwards.

It is not surprising, therefore, that in his theological reflections Edwards closely associated the natural world with the beauty of the Lord. As we have seen, he avoided the familiar theological notion that God created the world from nothing, *ex nihilo,* preferring to stress that creation emerged *ad extra* from the Lord's self-giving character. In one of his last published writings Edwards meditated on "the propensity in God to diffuse himself," concluding that such giving forth was a completion in God's nature, that God's personality would not have been realized without it.

> Thus that nature in a tree, by which it puts forth buds, shoots out branches, and brings forth leaves and fruit, is a disposition that terminates in its own complete self. And so the disposition in the sun to shine, or abundantly to diffuse its fulness, warmth, and brightness, is only a tendency to its own most glorious and complete state. So God looks on the communication of himself, and the emanation of his infinite glory, to belong to the fulness and completeness of himself; as though he were not in his most glorious state without it. Thus the church of Christ . . . is called the

fulness of Christ; as though he were not in his complete
state without her; like Adam without Eve.[4]

In some of his unpublished notes, Edwards searched
for words to explain why he experienced Christ distinctively
in natural settings. He suggested that "the beauties of nature
are really emanations or shadows of the excellencies of the
Son of God."[5] He did not mean that we might discover God by
looking at nature; he had no "natural theology" in this sense.
Nor did he mean that nature had no reality of its own but
was merely the shadow of some higher reality which remained out of sight. His Platonism drew him toward this second possibility, but I believe he was trying to express another
truth that emerged from personal experience. I will explain
this with some concepts Edwards himself did not use.

Replacing Edwards' Platonism with an ecological perspective, I have suggested that the world is a basic expression
of God's beauty, not an accidental or arbitrary creation. The
Lord as revealed in Scripture encourages living beings to
flower with individuality while contributing to the complex of
life. God's beauty is manifest to the believer in environments
where life and diversity flourish. In giving life to others, our
Lord graciously balances presence with reticence, support
with withdrawal, to permit living beings to find themselves.

We do not usually discover this biblical Lord through
contemplation of nature. However, once we have our own
experience of God's moral beauty, we may see God's beauty
confirmed in the natural world around us. Although God is
often elusive, and our feelings for the Lord may be difficult to
release, nature is vividly present. When we wish fresh experience of God, nature may assist us sacramentally.[6] Our sensual interplay with nature may help us release feelings toward
the Lord.

This was Edwards' experience. His delight in nature
awakened his feelings; thus aroused by beauty, he was able to
feel God's love and express his love for Christ. His Platonic
language veils, but does not hide, memories of many days
when nature served as his sacrament, when peace and joy in

the woods beyond Northampton helped him experience God's beauty and express delight in his Savior.

> So that when we are delighted with flowery meadows and gentle breezes of wind we may consider that we only see the emanations of the sweet benevolence of Jesus Christ. When we behold the fragrant rose and lily, we see his love, and purity. So the green trees and fields, and singing birds are the emanations of his infinite joy and benignity. The easiness and naturalness of trees and vines shadows of his infinite beauty and loveliness. The christal rivers and murmuring streams, have the footsteps of his sweet grace and beauty. When we behold the light and brightness of the sun, the golden edges of an evening cloud, or the beauteous bow we behold the adumbrations of his glory and goodness, and the blue skies of his mildness and gentleness. There are so many things wherein we may behold his awful majesty. In the sun in his strength, in comets, in thunder, in the hovering thunder clouds in ragged rocks, and the brows of mountains. That beauteous light with which the world is filled in a clear day is a lively shadow of his spotless holiness and happiness and delight in communicating himself and doubtless this is a reason that Christ is compared so often to these things and called by their names, as the Sun of Righteousness the morning star the Rose of Sharon and lily of the valley, the apple tree amongst the trees of the wood a bundle of myrrhe, a Roe, or a young hart. By this we may discover the beauty of many of those metaphores and similes which to an unphilosophical person do seem so uncouth.[7]

Of course, plain people in particular find such metaphors and similes delightful. The "unphilosophical" whom Edwards scorns in this notebook entry are the literal-minded, pedestrian, orthodox, and anxious divines who drove poetry out of Puritan rhetoric. They are, alas, Edwards himself in his public demeanor. He did not infuse his sermons with this delight in nature, nor did he help his parishioners draw sacramental nourishment from their daily experiences in the fields and forests surrounding Northampton.

A Christian ecological perspective does not need to cling to metaphors and similes. We can feel free to experience directly the beauties of nature and to rejoice in them for themselves, understanding that experiencing these beauties draws us closer to God's own delight in the world the Lord created and loves. We can enjoy the integrity of natural life while, aroused by beauty, we draw close to the Lord. We can enjoy the comprehensive sabbath, which brings all creation together in praise of the Creator.

*   *   *

I do not propose a "natural theology." Although experience of nature and environmental relationships may confirm and enrich our awareness of the beauty of the Lord, nature does not usually lead people to the Lord. Neither the complexities of nature nor its sensual quality is likely to lead modern imagination beyond nature itself, unless one already has an idea of God drawn from other experience. The biblical Lord has chosen to engage humanity more personally than through natural awe. God awakens us not just to mysteries of existence, but to moral beauty.

Nevertheless, there is an important exception to this general observation. When a person has a cultural image of the biblical Lord, but the normal channels of relationship are inhibited, nature may become a Christlike link. In the first book of this theology, I suggested that this was John Muir's experience. As a child Muir memorized much of the Bible, and as a young man he cared deeply about religion. But his father, a religious fanatic with a disturbed mind, had so tyrannized and abused him in the name of Christ that Muir could not respond to Christ and the church with love. Through several deeply religious experiences with nature this tension in Muir resolved into a unique perspective. Loving nature and living in striking intimacy with wilderness, he came to love the God whose beauty, benevolence, and moral character were confirmed to him by his experience of nature. And he undertook a prophetic vocation to persuade American society that all life was valued by God and that wilderness environments were as important as human culture. Whether Muir thought of himself as a Christian is unclear; he probably saw himself as an unconventional one. Nevertheless, I am convinced he performed a prophetic Christian ministry.[8]

In the modern era there are many others who appear to follow a path similar to Muir's. They may be alienated from Christianity or Judaism by personal trauma, or their background may isolate them from meaningful contact with these faiths. Yet experience of nature may awaken them to moral and religious sensitivity and may even lead them to recognize a God of moral purpose.

I have seen this happen several times among people deeply affected by some aspect of environmental crisis. One friend was raised in the church but discouraged by what she saw as empty piety. When strip mining threatened to engulf her family's land and her neighbors' as well, she organized the resistance in her region. Out of love for the land and fresh moral passion, she came to appreciate the passion of Christ—his moral courage and his suffering. Faith became whole again, supporting her in a long, difficult struggle.

* * *

To see Christ in nature is important for Christians. Nature does not usually lead humans to the Lord—that is not its function. However, Christ can lead modern believers to nature. We may see Christ standing with despoiled landscapes, abused animals, endangered species, and poisoned ecosystems.

> "When I was hungry, you gave me food; when thirsty, you gave me drink; when I was a stranger you took me into your home, when naked you clothed me; when I was ill you came to my help, when in prison you visited me." . . .
> "Lord, when was it that we saw you hungry and fed you, or thirsty and gave you drink? . . .When did we see you ill or in prison, and come to visit you?" . . .
> "I tell you this: anything you did for one of my brothers [and sisters] here, however humble, you did for me."
> (Matthew 25:35–40, NEB, alt.)

Today "hungry or thirsty or sick or in prison" extends to what is eroded or polluted or endangered or valued only for human use. I want to enlarge traditional Christian doctrine to make it plain that the world we are abusing is the body of our Lord—not in a metaphysical sense but in an ethical sense.

The Apostle Paul claimed that "In Christ God was reconciling the world to [God's] self " (2 Corinthians 5:19, RSV, alt.). John said that God gave Jesus to the world because "God loved the world so much" (John 3:16, NEB). When early Christians tried to explain Christ's work in terms of his nature or his "being," they concluded that Christ was fully God and yet fully human—each nature complete, each unconfused with the other. This expression translated Christ's act of reconciliation into the philosophical language of being.

While this early Christian formula addressed the reconciliation of God and humanity in Christ, it did not treat so precisely the reconciliation of God and the world, of which both Paul and John had spoken. However, I find it consistent both with biblical faith and with early Christian doctrine to highlight Jesus' earthly, material, and natural character as part of his human nature. Christ was fully God and also fully earth-nature-material-world; these two natures were each complete yet distinct from the other. Because Christ had an earthly nature, his humanity, he identified with the earth and drew nature into his saving work. For this reason Paul, who saw Christ as the new Adam, the first of God's new children, believed that "the creation waits with eager longing and for the revealing of the [children] of God" so we who are Christlike may heal nature's wounds inflicted by human sinfulness (Romans 8:19, RSV, alt.).

It is appropriate to identify the earth ethically with Christ, which can be done without confusing the material with the divine. It is not appropriate to identify the earth metaphysically with God. The Lord is God, but the earth is God's creation to which God imparted its own, material substance. I reject any pantheism, which suggests that the earth is God's body or that our perceptions of the earth are our primary guide to God's nature and character. The theological understanding expressed in the notion "Christ" preserves the distinction between God and the world as it spans the separation.

Our guide to Christ's nature and character is always the memory of Jesus. Jesus gave himself to reconcile the world to God, and to reconcile those living in the world to each other. I merely underscore that Jesus' desire for reconciliation, and God's intention, extend beyond the human community to the whole of life and creation.

Christians may see Christ in abused nature, suffering with threatened life that God loves. We may respond with respect and care for nature, confident that we serve Christ as we do so. When we enjoy the world and take delight in nature, we are neither wasting time nor being distracted from our moral purpose. We are exercising those same sensual capacities used in our experience of the Lord, and we are equipping ourselves with experience that helps us fulfill a principal purpose of human existence: to care for the world as agents of God's mercy.

21. *Ecology Fulfilled*

Love is the only motive sufficient to protect the world. When more people engage themselves, affectionately, with the natural life on this planet, the decisions necessary to protect the earth will appear desirable, rather than simply difficult. Because the changes required of human society, in order to give nature its due, will be so far-reaching and challenging, love is essential.

Campaigns for environmental protection are often built on fear—fear of the disaster which will ensue if we do not, for example, control pollutants or protect genetic diversity. Certainly, fear focuses our attention, and mobilizing our fear may be necessary to achieve political action. But fear eventually subsides; it is not human nature to continue anxious alertness indefinitely. When we cannot change a situation, we make an adjustment. We accept the danger, perhaps, repressing our fear. Or we may scapegoat, substituting an available target to blame for a problem hard to reach. However, I believe that love for the earth is a stronger motive than fear. It is more likely to generate creative action, and it is also more likely to persist through the long effort required for change.

Some Christians, when they take up the cause of environmental responsibility, may use this concern as a means to achieve other, repressive goals. Environmental restraint may appear to be an attractive modern equivalent to traditional Catholic asceticism or Protestant puritanism, and some persons may embrace environmentalism to pacify anxiety about greed, luxury, or sensuality. Nature is better served, however, when our desires are expressed. Lust for life can motivate care for the earth. If we cultivate a passion for luxuriant nature we may forego more of the synthetic luxuries that take so heavy a toll on the environment. Sensuality should be our partner, not our adversary.

When we cultivate our capacities to see, hear, taste, and smell; to feel, experience and respond; and to think with care, we will find that these skills relate us to nature, to fellow humans, and to the Lord. I do not recommend hedonism, which is seeking pleasure but hiding from pain; rather I urge taking the risks of pain as well as pleasure in order to experience life.

We can trust our perception of beauty, a remarkably useful gift which combines our sensual experience of the world with our intuition—the deepest associations from our life—to lead us into relationships with potential for meaning and moral purpose. Experiences of beauty enlarge us, pointing toward wholeness; they can also focus our desires, contributing to our identity. To trust beauty is to risk affectionate engagement with life. Perceiving beauty revives hope that a relationship may prove meaningful. Although we will make some mistakes, responding to beauty is likely to nourish both us and the world around us.

A decade ago, when I first grasped the significance of beauty in Edwards' thinking, I also began to give increasing weight, in my own daily life, to beautiful experiences. I take aesthetic perceptions seriously now, not only in my environmental reflections but also in my farm planning; they "pay off" in healthy land and in personal satisfaction as well. I also trust beauty in intimate relationships: though I can be distracted by the pretty, as the beauty of a relationship grows I find that I become more reliable. Furthermore, I trust my perception of beauty in sorting the many opportunities and enticements of modern culture: I spend more time with what I find useful, less with trash. As I attend to the beauty of the Lord, I discover warmth and subtlety, grace and freedom, that surprise and delight me.

* * *

Modern Western men and women need new experiences with nature. From fresh experience and new patterns of engagement, appropriate ethics can emerge. Delight in nature can reduce our need for things that damage the earth. Theologian Jürgen Moltmann suggested that "The more human beings discover the meaning of their lives in joy in existence, instead of in doing and achieving, the better they will be able to keep their economic, social and political history within bounds."[1] Similarly, biologist Charles Birch, writing with theologian John B. Cobb, Jr., argued that it is the quality of our experience of other life which gives that life value to us.

> As long as rights of animals are viewed as demands upon human beings which are costly to us, they are almost certain to give way in practice. Other animals will be respected only as they are genuinely experienced in a different way, and that change will involve a change in the way human beings experience themselves as well.[2]

New experience of nature begins with accepting our place in the community of life and regarding other creatures as members of this community also. It involves looking at other life for what it is, not simply for what it can do for humanity; respect for life needs to become the primary lens through which we view nature. Aldo Leopold suggested that even science can proceed from this motivation. The exercise of human power over nature, and "the idea of controlled environment," no longer need to dominate our perspective. Science can also function as an exercise of wonder, as "respect for workmanship in nature."[3]

It will help us to see nature differently if we relinquish hierarchical thinking, which many now call "patriarchal" thinking. Evolution did not produce a pyramid with humanity at the top, but rather a lush garden with us in the midst of all life. Species each have distinctive capacities, which are not necessarily inferior to ours in terms of the requirements of the species or their contributions to the system of life as a whole. While each species draws life from its surroundings, it also performs useful tasks which support the community of life. It may also contribute a unique intelligence, sensitivity, or another quality to the ecosystem it inhabits. The world would be less rich if there were not species with keener eyes than ours, some that hear sounds we cannot, and many with a sharper sense of smell, so the environment is known, used, and enjoyed more thoroughly.

We can see abundant evidence of intelligence when we look either at other species or at ecosystems as a whole. If we define intelligence as "wisdom for life," we avoid the definitions constructed to exalt humans in general or scientists in particular. Then we can see that nature is not stupid. Intelligence is manifest differently by different species. Although we think of intelligence as a quality in individual persons, in fact human intelligence is augmented by elaborate cultural systems that store information, the fruits of the reflection of others, and patterns of behavior derived from experience. In some other species, such as ants or bees, basic intelligence is socialized in the colony or hive itself. The individual is limited to routine functions, but the group is amazingly flexible and innovative.

Ecosystems can be seen as a level of intelligence, an integration of vast experience into a life-sustaining whole, with individual pieces of experience stored in the genes of participants and in their relationships. Often smarter than human culture, ecosystems may be more productive in ways humans cannot equal. When people disrupt ecosystems to convert them to agricultural systems, we damage nature's "intelligence"—the way nature has evolved wisdom for life. Plant geneticist Wes Jackson points out that when humans destroy the information stored in environmental relationships, we must substitute cultural information and apply more energy to compensate for the reduced efficiency of the system. "Usually much more energy is applied than cultural information," he writes, "and ecological capital is wasted or polluted."[4]

A century ago John Muir observed that "God takes

care of everything that is wild but he only half takes care of tame things."[5] When we bring lands under cultivation and domesticate plants and animals, we assume responsibilities for their welfare which were once discharged by other systems in the natural habitat. I do not think domestication is wrong or inappropriate, provided extensive areas of the wild are also protected. But for the benefits we receive, we add a great deal to our ethical obligations, as well as to our practical responsibilities. To look at domesticated lands, plants, and livestock from this perspective is to see them as members of the family of life toward whom we have assumed special responsibilities in return for special benefits. We can then set our functional relationships with other species in a context of moral understanding.[6]

*   *   *

New experience of nature can lead to fresh understanding of human vocation within nature. We can grow beyond the notion that nature exists to be raw material for human creativity, or the belief that the earth's life is fulfilled only through human action. We can relinquish images of the earth as a prison from which we must be delivered, or a testing ground to prepare us for more significant life elsewhere. We can, instead, discover our life within the family of living things.

I do not accept the conclusion that sophisticated human culture is inherently destructive, and must be disassembled by people who will then find true life in more primitive, organic relationships. Nor do I accept the dualism of "deep ecology" thinkers who believe that nature is the good but human culture, when it steps beyond the rhythms of nature, is evil.[7] I see instead that modern culture opens new opportunities for humanity to contribute to ecological vitality.

I believe that humanity can perform distinctive functions in the service of natural life: *awareness, creativity, and protection*. These are not exclusive functions in the sense that no other species participates in them. Yet I agree with Jürgen

Moltmann's suggestion that "in human knowledge of nature, nature really recognizes itself."[8]

To be *aware* of the beauty of nature is an important part of the human calling. Awareness helps nature know itself. Among earthly species, humanity has unique abilities to see reflectively and perceive self-consciously. If we do not view nature as "other," but take our place within the fellowship of earthly life, we can exercise these capacities as part of the biosphere to which we belong. Our seeing and knowing can contribute to nature's self-awareness, adding consciousness to the intricate ecology of life. Our understanding would then not detract from the "intelligence" of an ecosystem, but augment it. To the natural expressions we hear around us we may also add our own wonder and praise.

Human capacities to contribute to nature's self-awareness may be enhanced by modern culture. For the first time in world history, a large part of the human population does not engage personally with nature for survival, so their view of nature is not dominated by survival needs. Many people have an opportunity, therefore, to see nature in new ways. Furthermore, progress in scientific understanding of natural life gives knowledge, unavailable to previous generations, which can deepen our appreciation of nature. When we choose to stand within the fellowship of natural life, what we know becomes part of nature's resources for ecological self-understanding.

John Muir is my model for this type of awareness. When I wrote about him I suggested that "Yosemite was never more beautiful than when John Muir leapt its peaks and gazed upon it with knowing love and delight."

> We know some species have sensory capacities which humans lack. Indeed, there may be many more sensibilities in nature than we imagine. Similarly, with his reflective capacities, Muir could experience the relationships of the Douglas squirrel in ways the squirrel itself could not. Muir could see ecologically and historically, and he could be analytical; but he never allowed analysis to distance him from those with whom he communed.

Muir's presence with all his human faculties, his recognition of beauty, his delight and praise, enriched the ecology. Although never intrusive, Muir entered fully into the place and became part of the High Sierra's reflection upon itself, helping Yosemite rejoice in its own beauty.[9]

Humanity has an important vocation as part of the *creativity* of the earth. I have suggested that God's self-expression, the Lord's beauty, supports the flowering of other lives that manifest their own individuality while contributing to the life of all. Life evolves toward increasingly diverse and complex ecosystems which offer sustenance to species and opportunities for new creativity. Humanity has been a particularly creative species, and in human culture we have capabilities that enhance the potential of life on this earth. Urban societies rival natural ecosystems in complexity, but bear quite different fruit. Science adds to the earth's understanding, while human arts and letters vastly extend the expressiveness of life.

Cultural developments may be environmentally damaging when they are not disciplined by ethical awareness of human place within the fabric of natural life. But human culture adds exciting potential to life on earth nevertheless. "A species co-evolves with its environment," observe Charles Birch and John Cobb; " . . . There is no stable, harmonious nature to whose wisdom humanity should simply submit. . . . Human culture is an immensely important factor in ecology and one which necessarily introduces profoundly new elements into the web of life."[10]

The entire system of life on this earth is now intertwined with human culture; life depends upon our cultural self-discipline to avoid gross pollution or nuclear destruction. Wilderness, where natural life proceeds largely on its own terms, depends upon the same cultural self-discipline through which humanity recognizes wilderness, defines it, and limits human intrusion upon it. Once wilderness was simply there, but now, for wilderness to continue, human culture must affirm natural life.

The characteristics of life on a large portion of the earth's land surface have been shaped by human culture in general and by agriculture in particular. Sometimes culture and nature confront each other; sometimes they intertwine. Often human engagement with nature is unstable. When we harvest temporary benefits for human use, we often do so at the cost of long-term environmental decline. In some areas, however, productive relationships have been established between culture and nature to serve human needs while creating new landscapes of beauty and stability. Microbiologist René Dubos writes affectingly of such a region from his childhood in the Ile de France, north of Paris, a landscape "without any notable characteristics except those conferred upon it by several millennia of continuous human occupation," a land that "has remained very fertile, even though much of it has been in continuous use for more than two thousand years."[11]

Sometimes a society has recovered from destructive tendencies. The beautiful landscapes of southern England which today delight visitors were once ravaged by the enclosure, deforestation, and overgrazing which accompanied the early industrial revolution. Fortunately, this destruction was followed by generations of sensitive replanting and cultivation.[12]

The critical challenge today is to develop ethics of cultivation for the many landscapes where humanity and nature shape each other. The future of life on earth depends upon both the creativity and moral sensitivity of our engagement with nature. We are called to create new beauty to augment, not to deplete, the earth's capacity for life. "Civilized Nature," René Dubos suggested, "should be regarded not as an object to be preserved unchanged, not as one to be dominated and exploited, but rather as a kind of garden to be developed according to its own potentialities, in which human beings become what they want to be according to their own genius. Ideally, man and Nature should be joined in a nonrepressive and creative functioning order."[13] When we respect nature within our identity, as part of what gives our life meaning, we will be more likely to contribute to its life, less likely simply to exploit it.

The human calling to create, along with our ability to contribute awareness to the terrestrial ecosystem, implies our responsibility to *protect*. However, we can protect only what we are aware of. Spreading this awareness among more people will be as important as deepening our knowledge; the politics of protection depend upon increasing numbers of human beings who care.

The earth would not require our protection if humanity were not creative, for this human gift has vast and destructive side-effects. Protection involves disciplining our creativity to reduce these side-effects. Protection itself, though, is a creative endeavor. We cannot simply screen nature from damage; we also need to enter ecosystems imaginatively to protect their liveliness.

For example, atmospheric buildup of carbon dioxide and other gases from the burning of fossil fuels—the "greenhouse effect"—may continue to raise the earth's temperature even if corrective measures were undertaken immediately. "In the past few decades . . . greenhouse forcing of the climate system has increased rapidly; it is now 3 to 10 times greater than during the previous century," reports Dr. James Hansen of the National Aeronautics and Space Administration. "By the early 21st century the global temperature should have risen well above any level experienced in the past 100,000 years."[14] This could bring drought to many of the productive grain-belt areas of the world, while melt of polar ice caps might increase sea level one to three feet, reducing productive coastal wetlands. To reduce this threat will require protection of existing forests, which help regulate global rainfall. It may require rapid, imaginative substitution of solar technologies for much fossil fuel consumption on a worldwide basis. In addition, coping with the consequences may require managing ecosystems affected by increased heat, decreased rain, or rising sea levels, to develop viable, adaptive systems of life more rapidly than nature would without human intervention.

Environmental concern should make us wiser and

more prudent, but it will also draw us more deeply into environmental management. The protection of our environment is likely to be the most stimulating challenge to human creativity in the history of the species. We have built our nest in the tree of life; now we must save the tree.

* * *

There is no assurance that the human species will be successful in this, its most fundamental task. In fact, there are many reasons to fear that this may be the last generation, or nearly the last, to live on an earth which remains hospitable and beautiful. Nuclear war could so devastate the earth that the simple, mutated life forms which survived the dark winter would need to begin another evolutionary journey, probably without human companionship. Human life could prove to be the earth's major mistake, God's moral tragedy.

Scenarios for slower death are equally plausible. Ozone depletion, forest depletion, "greenhousing," toxic pollution, human crowding, and other threats yet unseen may combine to wither both the vitality of this planet and the joy of being alive.[15] Our grandchildren may not die. Instead they may live in a purgatory we bequeath them, suffering along with the lingering earth. A few, proud of their technology, may escape in spaceships to begin life anew elsewhere; but a species which had destroyed one planet of such magnificence would not be a promising addition to any other.

We may work to prevent this disastrous future. We may awaken and attempt to rouse our sisters and brothers. But what is our calling on the dark days when hope of success seems unreal? What can compensate for the pain that comes to us on those days because of our heightened sensitivity to the fragile, vulnerable beauty of the earth? I believe that when I perceive the beauty of a landscape I add something to that landscape which it desires: awareness. If it is the landscape on which I depend, I also add self-consciousness, for it and I are no longer separate.

Beauty is fulfilled in being seen, known, and experienced. Therefore, God created a beautiful world and created many species with open eyes, ears, and nostrils to experience it. In the days that we have, it is important to enter this communion, so that we and the earth may love each other and praise God together.

22. *Death in the Okavango*

It took us two days to drive across Botswana from the capital, Gaborone, to Maun on the edge of the Okavango Delta. The landscape, which ranges from arid grasslands to bone-dry desert, supports only one million people in an area four-fifths the size of Texas. Botswana is a black-ruled, parliamentary democracy, nearly surrounded by white-ruled South Africa and Namibia which South Africa occupies. My wife Anne and I were taking a trip with friends who represent Church World Service in southern Africa. It was April 1986.

As we drove we could see the ravages of recent drought and overgrazing. For centuries the tribal people have kept cattle as their principal wealth. Until recently, people and cattle lived in nomadic harmony with the land, searching for grass and water just as the abundant wildlife of the region did. The dryland grasses, rich in protein, supported unusually fine beef, most of which is now exported to western Europe. I raise grass-fed beef myself, and I found Botswana steaks especially tasty.

But now the grasses are disappearing, since drought has accelerated a trend rooted in cultural changes. As nomadic patterns have been displaced in this century by claims to private property and the delineation of communal lands, cattle have been restricted to specific ranges. At the insistence of the European Economic Community and with financing from the World Bank, the whole country is being crisscrossed by veterinary control fences designed to block cattle migration, in hopes of limiting the spread of hoof and mouth disease. An unintended side effect of these fences has been the death of tens of thousands of antelopes, wildebeests, and other animals who perish from thirst or starvation when they meet a fence that cuts off their migration route. As game has diminished, cattle herds have increased. When the season is dry and they cannot range widely, cattle trample the grass toward extinction.

Twenty species of large, herbivorous mammals recently grazed these plains—antelope, impala, Cape buffalo, zebra, wildebeest, warthog, elephant, giraffe, and others. Each had its favorite plants and instinctive migration patterns. Together they grew two to eight times as much flesh as cattle can from the same landscape, while the variety in their appetites and migratory habits put less stress on the arid plant communities.[1] Now, in some areas, palatable grasses can be found only beneath the protective thorn bushes that are spreading across the former grasslands.

From Maun our group took a small plane into the Okavango Delta, landing on a sand airstrip that ran the spine of a small island. The Okavango River is the only major river in the world which does not reach a body of water. Instead, after flowing southeast from headwaters in Angola, it spreads its triangular delta over 6,000 square miles on the edge of the Kalahari Desert. As the waters flow toward the desert, they evaporate or seep into the sands.

The delta is one of the world's most beautiful and unusual landscapes. Less than a third comprises low-lying, sandy islands covered with dense grasses that are interrupted occasionally by a solitary baobab tree or groves of acacia, palm, and other African trees, forming shapes exotic to an American visitor. Here the full range of African mammals graze, including the lechwe, tsessebe, steenback, reedbuck, and kudu, in addition to the more familiar ones. They, in turn, draw predators—the jackal, wild dog, hyena, leopard, lion, and cheetah.

Another third of the delta is permanent streams and swamps. Hippo graze channels through tall stands of reeds and papyrus, making openings for water to flow. Crocodiles, too, share these waters with the many species of fish. The waters are shallow, crystal clear, and pure to drink. Natives stand in the stern of *mekoro,* dugout canoes, as they pole themselves and visitors through the channels.

The largest third is subject to seasonal fluctuation, dry in May but inundated by August as the annual flood arrives from Angola. Accompanying the slow, southeasterly movement of floodwaters are magnificent flocks of birds—hundreds of species including storks, pelicans, eagles, hawks, ducks, and herons. The birds, most of all, have brought fame to the Okavango. There are birds at all times of the year, but when the flood waters churn the insects and fish, the largest flocks are drawn to the delta. As fish, birds, and reptiles advance, mammals retreat to dry ground.

The Okavango is a miracle of life. The sandy soil holds few nutrients, and few wash from Angola into the clear waters of the Okavango. Only sunshine is abundant. Thanks to sunshine and to the instability of seasonal rising and falling water, a remarkably complex ecosystem has formed. No one species is predominantly abundant. Any particular species of mammal, bird, fish, or reptile can be found in higher concentrations elsewhere in Africa. But almost everything that lives in Africa is present in the Okavango. Each has found a place in this intricate meeting of earth, air, and water.

The annual flood provides the basis for this uncommonly rich, diverse ecosystem. A terrestrial life system shares much of the area with an aquatic life system, while insects and birds thrive on the ever-changing margins between these two. As the annual flood churns up the web of life, species become more available—and more vulnerable—to each other.

The sense of abundant life was overwhelming to me. It was like a visit to the Garden of Eden. Each morning we gathered at sunrise on the river bank, and our two native guides poled us in *mekoro* across to Chief's Island to walk and observe wildlife. They insisted we walk in single file with the older man, Batswelelwa, in the lead and the other in the rear. One carried a hatchet in case we met lions. Batswelelwa was lean, erect, and strikingly alert. He seemed to hear every sound, notice every movement. After motioning us with a graceful hand to be still, he would lean around a bush or giant anthill at the edge of the woods to peer across a grassy expanse. If he saw animals or birds of interest, he would bring us forward quietly and help us observe without calling attention to ourselves. The quiet of these walks helped me enter the space where animals and birds lived.

Later in the day we would be poled up stream or down, passing through beautiful reeds and plants, watching birds, and occasionally a crocodile. On a sand bar with good visibility, where crocodiles could not lurk, we might swim. We never saw hippos though we often saw where they had been. Once, in a small boat, we rested quietly next to reeds where we could hear—but not see—hippos eating. Since hippos that see boats may get angry and try to tip them over, I was content that we did not see each other.

One morning we set out walking across Chief's Island with particular determination. We wanted to find giraffes, which we had not yet seen. I felt more at home on the island now, but as we walked through stands of tall grass I meditated on lions. We had seen no lions, though there were some in the area. They were the danger most feared, since they were likely to see a person before they themselves were seen. Tall grass was their special habitat. Actually, more people are injured by Cape buffalo, which graze in herds like cattle but can charge angrily. We had met them without alarm. Meeting a lion while on foot, however, was another matter.

Although I hoped we would not meet, I realized I was nevertheless quite willing to take the risk for the beauty of this experience on Chief's Island. It is more dangerous to

drive the interstate at home, I thought—even more dangerous to walk the streets of New York, a city I love. I have had
some courage in danger, but I have always dreaded that I
might die pointlessly, struck down by a truck with brake
failure, for example, or mugged by a stranger. Walking
through the tall grass, thinking about lions, I did not feel
that the death threatened here would be pointless. I would
nourish a fine creature. I would enter the cycle of life and
death in a beautiful place.

My hope for my death has been that I might die elder-
ly and peaceful in my own bed or, as second choice, die in
honor for a cause in which I believe. Now, however, a third
fantasy came to mind. If stricken with cancer and given six
months to live, I might well choose—after other events of
love, delight, and reunion—to walk out on Chief's Island and
look for a lion. How much more I might enjoy the lion than
the ministrations of some hospital staff with their radiation
therapy, intravenous tubes, and pain-killing drugs. I will
remember Chief's Island.

Fortunately, we did not meet a lion that morning.
Instead we met a family of five giraffes—three adults and
two youths—splotched pale yellow and green-brown, gently
outlined among the trees as they nibbled the leaves, graceful as they loped away. Then we met a family of seven,
equally beautiful, and saw them again and again as we
quietly circled.

* * *

During our stay in the Okavango, I saw no deaths
more violent than a fish eagle snatching a fish from the
stream, yet I was impressed here as nowhere else by how life
depends upon death. When I farm the soils of Virginia I can
easily imagine that life is more a chemical process than a biological one; the cycles of life and death within the soil involve
creatures too small to call attention to themselves. But in the
Okavango it was clear that all life built on other life.

The hippos that grazed the channels, devouring the

reeds, also fertilized the waters with manure which, after digestion by other organisms, provided food for fish. The trees and grasses on the islands lived from the decaying remains of their predecessors. Grasses were foraged by a greater variety of mammals than I had ever seen in one place, while giraffes and elephant foraged the trees. The variety of animals protected the diversity of grasses, bushes, and trees; the grazing pressure was not too great on any one. Predators, in turn, fed from the grazing animals. Culling the old and the weak, keeping the herds moving, they helped the population live within its environment without destroying the vegetation upon which it depends. The yearly flood also kept everything in motion, first expanding the swamp and then, in retreat, extending the landscape.

An amazing variety of plants and trees, insects and reptiles, fish and birds, animals and humans, found an opportunity for life. But with such an opportunity comes a responsibility to die and contribute oneself, however reluctantly, to nourish other life. The death of each creature is essential to the life of others. Withdraw the results of death from the environment—by cutting trees and hauling them away, or by harvesting too many animals, crocodiles, or fish—and the complex balance of life might begin to disintegrate.

As a Christian I am challenged by this insight. Christians have been taught that death is alien to life. We are told that death was introduced into the world by human sin. So many times, at funerals, I have attempted to comfort mourners with the Apostle Paul's words:

> But now is Christ risen from the dead, and become the firstfruits of them that slept. For since by man came death, by man came also the resurrection of the dead. . . . For he must reign, till he hath put all enemies under his feet. The last enemy that shall be destroyed is death.
>
> (1 Corinthians 15:20–21, 25–26, KJV)

Now I think that death may be part of the goodness of God's creation, so long as death and life remain in balance with each other. To eat, and finally to be eaten, are part of the blessing of God. Certainly, human sinfulness can make death alien, as when one murders another. We might also extend our understanding of murder to include human abuse of other species and systems of life. Particular circumstances can make death tragic. Christ rose to overcome abusive death and to mitigate tragic death. However, death at the completion of a full life of love, experience, and expression is not tragic. It is a gift. Death is a way we give life to each other within the biosphere we share.

During the years when Darwin was developing his theory of evolution, Alfred Tennyson, who would become poet laureate to the imperial court of Queen Victoria, brooded over the apparent contradiction between the loftiness of human sensibilities and the viciousness of nature.

> Man, her [Nature's] last work, who seem'd so fair
> Such splendid purpose in his eyes. . .
>
> . . . .
>
> Who trusted God was love indeed
> And love Creation's final law—
> Tho' Nature, red in tooth and claw
> With ravine, shriek'd against his creed . . .[2]

In the twentieth century some of us have developed both a new appreciation for nature and a more modest appraisal of human sensibilities. Compared to human destructiveness, nature seems benign. Death comes to each, and sometimes death is bloody and painful. Nevertheless, those who graze the wild, as in the Okavango, appear to spend most of their hours in alert contentment. Perhaps they know joys and satisfactions which balance the moments of pain. Certainly they are happier than their cousins who die slowly of thirst along the veterinary control fences.

Natural systems are benign compared to the cruelties inflicted on them by human culture—even culture at its best. Botswana is still a poor, "underdeveloped" country. Yet even in Botswana no natural force—not natural predation, not years of drought—has had such cruel consequences as human eagerness for political definition, private property, personal wealth, and medical manipulation of nature. These goals are among the things we desire most, and they often have genuine value. Yet even the best in human culture may destroy the world unless we recognize nature from the depths of our personal identity, unless we build understanding and respect for nature into the core of our culture.

*   *   *

Less than one quarter of the Okavango Delta, the part within the Moremi Wildlife Reserve, is protected by law. The tsetse fly has preserved the wilderness character of the rest. The bite of this bloodsucking fly carries sleeping sickness to humans and a related infection to domestic livestock. Both are fatal if not treated. Among the human settlement in the Okavango, treatment for sleeping sickness is now available, and as a result the fatality rate is low. Cattle grazing, however, remains impractical. This is the only reason why large areas of the Okavango have not been environmentally degraded and grazed heavily like most of Botswana. A fly has been an effective guardian of the wilderness.

In Maun we saw four-engine cargo planes take off to pass low, back and forth across the delta. These planes spray pesticides designed to kill the tsetse fly: endosulphan, deltemethryn, or aldrin. Another, dieldrin, is sprayed by hand from the ground. The program is financed through the United Nations Food and Agriculture Organization which has a campaign to eliminate the tsetse fly from Africa and thus extend the range for livestock. The pesticides are somewhat toxic to other insects and may injure fish, birds, and mammals—just how dangerous they are is in dispute.[3]

The greatest danger, however, is that the program might succeed. According to Botswana conservationists, a decade after the tsetse fly disappears from the Okavango, herdsmen and their cattle will be pervasive. The grass will be quickly depleted, as will the wild animals, the birds, and the fish. The beauty will disappear. People will be hungry again, and the world will be poorer.

Humanity still finds it easier to exterminate competing life than to learn how to live with nature. Since we do not accept death in our culture, we inflict it upon the world.

The lion may be gone before I need her.

Suggestions for Reading

There are beautiful books which stimulate our perception of the natural world. Aldo Leopold, *A Sand County Almanac* (San Francisco and New York: Sierra Club/ Ballantine, 1972) is a splendid treasury of natural observation and ethical insight. John Muir's writings remain engaging. Start with the intimate collection of diaries and letters, *To Yosemite and Beyond*, ed. Robert Engberg and Donald Wesling (Madison, WI: University of Wisconsin Press, 1980); then consult my reading suggestions at the end of *Baptized into Wilderness*, Book 1 of this series. An excellent recent book by Barry Lopez, *Arctic Dreams: Imagination and Desire in a Northern Landscape* (New York: Charles Scribner's Sons, 1986), is filled with sight and insight.

Jonathan Edwards is an acquired taste for the modern reader. Because his language is archaic and his style is sometimes tedious, it takes persistence to engage with his amazing mind. *Selections*, edited and introduced by Clarence H. Faust and Thomas H. Johnson (New York: Hill and Wang, 1962), presents extracts from all his principal works, including his charming youthful writings. It has a useful introduction to his life. Students of Edwards will want to consult the fine critical volumes of *Works of Jonathan Edwards* published by Yale University Press. A collection of Edwards' writings from *The Great Awakening* (ed. C. C. Goen, 1972) and his seminal work on *Religious Affections* (ed. John E. Smith, 1959) may be found in this series.

We need a good, modern biography of Jonathan

Edwards. Ola Elizabeth Winslow won a Pulitzer Prize forty years ago for *Jonathan Edwards* (New York: Collier Books, 1961), but the biography is not adequate to the complexity of the man or to the movement he led. Perry Miller's analysis of Edwards' ideas, *Jonathan Edwards* (William Sloan Associates, 1949) is more stimulating, and includes good biographical sketches. William A. Clebsch views Edwards from an unusual perspective in *American Religious Thought, A History* (Chicago: University of Chicago Press, 1973), tracing a philosophical line from Edwards to Emerson to William James. Edwards' philosophical Platonism is emphasized in Roland André Delattre's, *Beauty and Sensibility in the Thought of Jonathan Edwards: An Essay in Aesthetics and Theological Ethics* (New Haven: Yale University Press, 1968), a book rich with insight.

Wilhelm Reich's life and thought are now accessible to the lay reader thanks to Myron Sharaf's brilliant, engaging biography, *Fury on Earth* (New York: St. Martin's Press, 1983). Most of Reich's major writings are in print. To read him directly, I suggest you start with *The Function of the Orgasm* (New York: Simon and Schuster, 1973). Edward W. L. Smith, in *The Body in Psychotherapy* (Jefferson, NC: McFarland & Co., 1985), provides an excellent current statement of the humanistic approach to psychotherapy which derives from Reich.

For the Christian reader, the most provocative approach to Erik Erikson's thought is *Young Man Luther* (New York: W. W. Norton and Company, 1958), where you can see his psychobiographical method concerning a life already familiar. *Childhood and Society* (New York: W. W. Norton and Company, Inc., 1963) includes the most systematic presentation of Erikson's theory of psychosocial development leading to identity formation. Do not miss *Gandhi's Truth: On the Origins of Militant Nonviolence* (New York: W. W. Norton and Company, Inc., 1969), Erikson's most beautiful book, which won the National Book Award and Pulitzer Prize.

Keith Thomas, in *Man and the Natural World: A History of the Modern Sensibility* (New York: Pantheon Books, 1983), provides a delightful summary of English attitudes toward nature from Medieval times to the present. Donald Worster writes with unusual moral sensitivity about Henry David Thoreau and Charles Darwin in *Nature's Economy: A History of Ecological Ideas* (Cambridge: Cambridge University Press, 1985). British philosopher Mary Midgley takes a tough, clear look at the abuse of evolutionary ideas in *Evolution as a Religion* (London: Methuen & Co., 1985). Donald R. Griffin has written an important book on the intelligence of other creatures, *Animal Thinking* (Cambridge, MA: Harvard University Press, 1984).

Good theological writing about nature, from a Christian perspective, is still scarce. H. Paul Santmire provides a useful historical review in *The Travail of Nature: The Ambiguous Ecological Promise of Christian. Theology* (Philadelphia: Fortress Press, 1985). In Christian history, Francis of Assisi is the most prophetic voice for nature. Edward A. Armstrong has written a critical and engaging study, *Saint Francis: Nature Mystic: The Derivation and Significance of the Nature Stories in the Franciscan Legend* (Berkeley: University of California Press, 1973). The title essay in Rosemary Radford Ruether, *New Woman / New Earth* (New York: Seabury Press, 1983), is particularly stimulating. Walter Brueggemann's *The Land* (Philadelphia: Fortress Press, 1977) is a pioneering biblical study in this field. The most careful systematic attempt to give nature new prominence in Christian theology is Jürgen Moltmann's *God in Creation: A New Theology of Creation and the Spirit of God* (San Francisco: Harper & Row, 1985), although Moltmann's excellent insights are limited by an academic tone which seems distant from experience of nature. A biologist, Charles Birch, and a theologian, John B. Cobb, Jr., have written *The Liberation of Life: From the Cell to the Community* (Cambridge: Cambridge University Press, 1981), based on the process philosophy of Charles Hartshorne, which here yields a hierarchy of moral value. Albert J. Fritsch, Jesuit priest and Appalachian activist, has poured forth books on environmental responsibility: the most charming is the terse devotional, *Appalachia: A Meditation* (Chicago: Loyola University Press, 1986), with fine photographs by Warren E. Brunner.

Notes

Introduction

1. *Science*, Lynn White, Jr. "The Historical Roots of Our Ecologic Crisis," 10 March 1967, 1203–1207. This essay has been widely reprinted.
2. Aldo Leopold, *A Sand County Almanac* (San Francisco and New York: Sierra Club/Ballantine, 1972), 246.
3. John D. "Jay" Rockefeller IV was one of the leaders who asked me to take this role. During his first campaign for governor he ran on the promise to abolish strip mining in this state, historically dominated by the coal industry. He was defeated. Four years later, chastened, he ran for governor promising support for "responsible" strip mining, and won election with the help of the coal industry.
4. The briefing papers that I prepared for Hechler were published in 1971 by the Sierra Club as *The Strip Mining of America: An Analysis of Surface Coal Mining and the Environment*—the first book on the subject from an environmental perspective. Later the Methodist Church asked me to write *SPOIL: A Moral Study of Strip Mining for Coal* (New York: Board of Global Ministries, The United Methodist Church, 1976).
5. "*Theology:* The study of the nature of God and religious truth; rational inquiry into religious questions, especially those posed by Christianity." (*The American Heritage Dictionary of the English Language* [Boston: Houghton Mifflin, 1970]).
6. Perry Miller, *Jonathan Edwards* (n.p.: William Sloane Associates, 1949), 309.
7. William A. Clebsch, *American Religious Thought: A History* (Chicago: University of Chicago Press, 1973), xvi.
8. John Passmore, *Man's Responsibility for Nature: Ecological Problems and . . . Western Traditions* (London: Gerald Duckworth & Co., Ltd., 1974), 188–189.

Part I. Beauty

Chapter 1. Approaching Beauty

1. Alan Paton, *Cry, the Beloved Country* (New York: Charles Scribner's Sons, 1948), 3–4.

2. *The American Heritage Dictionary*, definition of "beautiful."

3. *The American Heritage Dictionary*, definition of "beauty."

4. Plotinus, *The Enneads*, 5.8.9, quoted in Roland André Delattre, *Beauty and Sensibility in the Thought of Jonathan Edwards: An Essay in Aesthetics and Theological Ethics* (New Haven: Yale University Press, 1968), 28.

5. Immanuel Kant, quoted in Hannah Arendt, *Lectures on Kant's Political Philosophy* (Chicago: University of Chicago Press, 1982), 30.

6. Arendt, *Lectures on Kant's Political Philosophy*, 30.

Chapter 2. Taste and See

1. "A Divine and Supernatural Light" in Jonathan Edwards, *Representative Selections*, Clarence H. Faust and Thomas H. Johnson (New York: Hill and Wang, 1962), 108. "A Treatise on Grace," quoted in Delattre, *Beauty and Sensibility*, 50, n. 22.

2. William T. Davis, ed., *Bradford's History of the Plymouth Plantation* (New York: Charles Scribner's Sons, 1908), 96.

3. Kantian philosopher Hannah Arendt also noticed these characteristics of taste.

> The most surprising aspect of this business is that common sense, the faculty of judgment and of discriminating between right and wrong, should be based on the sense of taste. . . . Smell and taste give inner sensations that are entirely private and incommunicable. . . . One can withhold judgment from what one sees and, though less easily, one can withhold judgment from what one hears or touches. But in matters of taste or smell, the it-pleases-or-displeases-me is immediate and overwhelming.
>
> *Lectures on Kant's Political Philosophy*, 64.

4. Jonathan Edwards, *The Nature of True Virtue* (Ann Arbor: University of Michigan Press, Ann Arbor Paperback, 1960), 98–99. Perceiving harmony might indeed entail reflection, but taking pleasure in a tune does not.

5. Karl Barth, quoted in *Religion and Culture*, ed. Walter Leibrecht (New York: Harper and Brothers, 1959), 64.

6. Jonathan Edwards, *Religious Affections*, ed. John E. Smith, vol. 2 of *Works of Jonathan Edwards* (New Haven: Yale University Press, 1959), 272.

7. Edwards, "A Divine and Supernatural Light" in *Selections*, 108.

8. John Muir, from "The Glacier Meadows of the Sierra," quoted

in Michael P. Cohen, *The Pathless Way: John Muir and American Wilderness* (Madison, Wisconsin: University of Wisconsin Press, 1984), 216.

9.   Edwards, *Nature of True Virtue*, 88.

10. Edwards, *Nature of True Virtue*, 5.

Chapter 3. Ecology

1.   Francis Bacon, quoted in Lewis Mumford, *The Pentagon of Power* (New York: Harcourt Brace Jovanovich, 1970), 118. Mumford gives an excellent review of Bacon's influence on the development of science and of the culture which supports technology.

2.   Fraser Darling, "A Wider Environment of Ecology and Conservation," in *America's Changing Environment,* ed. Roger Revelle and Hans H. Landsberg (Boston: Houghton Mifflin, 1970), 3. In another definition, Ramon Margalef defines ecology as

> the study of systems at a level in which individuals or whole organisms may be considered elements of interaction, either among themselves, or with a loosely organized environmental matrix. Systems at this level are named ecosystems and ecology is the biology of ecosystems.

Quoted in Robert Leo Smith, *The Ecology of Man: An Ecosystem Approach* (New York: Harper & Row, 1972), 4.

3.   Donald Worster, in *Nature's Economy: A History of Ecological Ideas* (Cambridge: Cambridge University Press, 1985), 256ff., clarifies in detail the distinctions between what he calls the "utilitarian" and "organic" ecologists.

4.   S. Dillon Ripley and Helmut K. Buechner, "Ecosystem Science as a Point of Synthesis," *America's Changing Environment*, ed. Revelle and Landsberg, 24.

5.   Leopold, *A Sand County Almanac*, xviii–xix.

6.   Paul Shepard and Daniel McKinley, eds., *The Subversive Science: Essays Toward an Ecology of Man* (Boston: Houghton Mifflin, 1969), 9.

7.   Leopold, *Sand County Almanac*, 137, 139–140.

8.   Durward Allen, "Our Wildlife Legacy," quoted in Frank Graham, Jr., "A Clear-eyed View of the Natural World," *Audubon*, March 1985, 99.

9.   Edwards, "Of Insects," in *Selections*, 10.

Chapter 4. The Beauty of the Lord

1.   Edwards, *Religious Affections,* 298.

2. "Beauty" is the rendering in the King James Version and in versions derived from the KJV, such as the New English Bible and the Revised Standard Version. Interestingly, the Jerusalem Bible selects another of Edwards' favorite words and renders the phrase "to enjoy the sweetness of Yahweh." The Hebrew word behind these translations is not the word used for physical beauty. It has a connotation which includes "delightfulness" and "pleasantness" (Terrien), "graciousness" (Weiser), "kindness," and "agreeableness" (Landes). Each of these renderings suggests the characteristics I stress. Beauty is not a static quality, contained within the one to whom it is attributed. It is a quality of engagement and relationship. See Samuel Terrien, *The Psalms and Their Meaning for Today* (Indianapolis: Bobbs-Merrill, 1952), 213, 217; and Artur Weiser, *The Psalms: A Commentary* (Philadelphia: Westminster Press, 1962), 248. George Landes' comment was in conversation with the author.

3. Whenever I change language in a version, the footnote citation includes "alt.," indicating alteration. See Book 3, Chapters 8 and 9, for a discussion of sexuality in relation to God.

4. From "Miscellanies," No. 293 in the Yale Collection of Edwards' manuscripts (Yale University Library). Quoted in Delattre, *Beauty and Sensibility*, 152.

5. Edwards, Misc. 247, quoted in Delattre, *Beauty and Sensibility*, 177.

6. Edwards, Misc. 1151, quoted in Delattre, *Beauty and Sensibility*, 177.

Part II. Landscapes of the Mind

1. Lisel Mueller, "Monet Refuses the Operation," in *Fifty Years of American Poetry* (New York: Harry N. Abrams, Inc., 1984) 202–203.

Chapter 6. Projection

1. See Edward W. L. Smith, *The Body in Psychotherapy* (Jefferson, NC: McFarland & Co., Inc., 1985), 39, for a discussion of projection and other pathologies which cloud awareness.

2. Stephen J. Pyne, *Dutton's Point: An Intellectual History of the Grand Canyon* (n.p.: Grand Canyon Natural History Association, 1982), Monograph No. 5.

3. See also Psalm 145:10–16, Exodus 23:10–12, Hosea 4:1–3. I will develop a biblical understanding of the relationships between God, humanity, and nature in Book 3 of this series.

4. The Stoics had taught the same: nature existed solely to serve man's interests (Aristotle, *Politics*, 1256a–b; Cicero, *De Natura Deorum*, ii.14, 61–65; as cited in Keith Thomas, *Man and the Natural World, a History of the Modern Sensibility* [New York: Pantheon Books, 1983], 17).

5. Francis Bacon, vi. 747, quoted in Thomas, *Man and the Natural World*, 18.

6. Thomas, *Man and the Natural World*, 33.

7. This contrasted with the Old Testament perspective that the *nephesh*, "spirit" or "breath," is given by God to humans and animals, but not to plants (See Genesis 1:30).

8. Plato, *Republic*, 571, quoted in Thomas, *Man and the Natural World*, 36.

9. Thomas, *Man and the Natural World*, 41.

10. Sir Thomas Pope Blount, *A Natural History* (1693), sig. A6, quoted in Thomas, *Man and the Natural World*, 43.

11. Thomas, *Man and the Natural World*, 106.

12. Thomas, *Man and the Natural World*, 220–221.

13. Thomas Edwards, *Gangraena* (1646), i.20, quoted in Thomas, *Man and the Natural World*, 166.

14. Quoted in Thomas, *Man and the Natural World*, 189.

15. I will further analyze modern agricultural perspectives toward the land in Book 4 of this series.

16. Thomas, *Man and the Natural World*, 184.

17. From John Wesley Powell's journal, quoted in *The Grand Canyon, Early Impressions*, ed. Paul Schullery (Boulder, CO: Colorado Associated University Press, 1981), 13.

Chapter 7. London, 1842

1. Charles Darwin, Letter to Charles Lyell in 1841, quoted in Worster, *Nature's Economy*, 147.

2. Friedrich Engels, *The Condition of the Working Class in England*, quoted in Worster, *Nature's Economy*, 148.

3. Darwin, quoted in Worster, *Nature's Economy*, 125.

4. Darwin's journal, quoted in Worster, *Nature's Economy*, 123.

5. Herman Melville, "The Encantadas, or 'Enchanted Isles,' " quoted in Worster, *Nature's Economy*, 120–121.

6. Darwin's "Autobiography," quoted in Worster, *Nature's Economy*, 149.

7. Darwin, quoted in Worster, *Nature's Economy*, 128.

8. I have omitted the important role played by Herbert Spencer,

who devised the term "evolution" before Darwin did, who simplified and popularized notions of biological struggle for survival, and who is primarily responsible for the application of these biological images to the social analysis which came to be called "Social Darwinism." Mary Midgley brilliantly appraises Spencer's influence, and defends Darwin, in *Evolution as a Religion: Strange Hopes and Stranger Fears* (London: Methuen & Co. Ltd., 1985).

9. Worster, *Nature's Economy*, 154.
10. Darwin, quoted in Worster, *Nature's Economy*, 161.
11. Darwin, quoted in Worster, *Nature's Economy*, 147.
12. Karl Marx, letter of 18 June, 1862, quoted in Thomas, *Man and the Natural World*, 90.
13. Marx, quoted in Thomas, *Man and the Natural World*, 23.
14. "Dogs and horses, Friedrich Engels would say . . . had so learned to understand human beings that 'anyone who has much to do with such animals will hardly be able to escape the conviction that there are plenty of cases where they now feel their inability to speak is a defect, although unfortunately it can no longer be remedied, owing to the vocal cords being too specialized in a definite direction.' " (Thomas, *Man and the Natural World*, 97).
15. Thomas, *Man and the Natural World*, 50 n.

Chapter 8. Affections

1. Taylor Stoehr, from his introduction to *Nature Heals: The Psychological Essays of Paul Goodman* (New York: Free Life Editions, 1977), p. xxii. Paul Goodman helped Fritz Perls formulate "Gestalt Therapy": together they wrote a book by that name in 1950. Gestalt was influenced by Wilhelm Reich, with whom both Perls and Goodman had worked. I introduce Reich later in this chapter and use his thought in the next chapter.
2. Edwards, *Religious Affections*, 101.
3. Edwards, *Freedom of the Will*, ed. Paul Ramsey, vol. 1 of *Works of Jonathan Edwards* (New Haven: Yale University Press, 1957), 142.
4. Edwards, *Freedom of the Will*, 144.
5. Edwards, *Religious Affections*, 97.
6. Edwards, *Religious Affections*, 272; "A Divine and Supernatural Light," in *Selections*, 108.
7. Reich also made the theological claims that orgone energy was the scientific equivalent of both God and "ether." However, I

will not deal further with Reich's biophysical theory of orgone energy. It is first of all a scientific theory, subject to scientific scrutiny and verification, and only derivatively a theory with metaphysical implications. The scientific community has not chosen to scrutinize Reich's experiments. Reich's heirs and orthodox disciples have perpetuated some of his paranoia. By refusing to release Reich's private experimental notes, they have made scientific scrutiny of his theory difficult. I have no competence to evaluate Reich's claims from a scientific perspective, although I think it is a profound shame that they are not being evaluated, because there might be some truth in them. Furthermore, I believe that while theology should be aware of contemporary physics, it is unwise to derive theology from any theory in physics. Energy theories, in my judgment, make poor theology.

Chapter 9. Insensibility

1. Jesus' quote is from Isaiah 6:9–10. The whole passage may illustrate a curious insensitivity on the part of the disciples. As recounted by Matthew (13:10–17), Mark (4:10–12), and Luke (8:9–10), who all depend on a common source for the story, the point seems to be that Jesus spoke to the crowd in parables in order to keep them from understanding, but explained things plainly to his disciples later. It seems far more likely that Jesus was explaining to his disciples that he spoke in parables to the crowd because parables appeal to the human affections more than statements in discursive language. Nevertheless, the crowd could not respond to the more affecting parables, Jesus concludes, whereas the disciples were sufficiently open to permit him to talk "straight" (discursively) to them on occasion. It would appear, however, that this explanation was misunderstood by the one who passed it on to the writers of the Gospels.

2. Wilhelm Reich, *The Murder of Christ* (New York: Farrar, Straus and Giroux, 1953), 63.

3. Wilhelm Reich, *Function of the Orgasm*, 7.

4. Reich, *Function of the Orgasm*, 7.

5. Reich, *Function of the Orgasm*, 201.

6. My three diagrams are based on Reich's diagrams in *Function of the Orgasm*, 142, 143.

7. Reich, *Function of the Orgasm*, 233.

8. Gandhi, quoted in Erik H. Erikson, *Gandhi's Truth: On the Origins of Militant Nonviolence* (New York: W.W. Norton & Co., Inc., 1969), 374. Gandhi applied the same insight to his

advocacy of sexual abstinence. "*Brahmacharya* consists in refraining from sexual indulgence, but we do not bring up our children to be impotent. They will have observed *brahmacharya* only if though possessed of the highest virility they can master the physical urge" (374). Indeed Gandhi had an abiding concern that the spread of his teaching not be an occasion for the repression of natural instincts in children.

> It is a difficult thing to teach them to defend themselves and yet not be overbearing. Till now, we used to teach them not to fight back if anyone beat them. Can we go on doing so now? What will be the effect of such teaching on a child? Will he, in his youth, be a forgiving or a timid man? My powers of thinking fail me. Use yours. . . . I have not found one master-key for all the riddles" (376).

9. A more complete version of the bodily parts saying is found in Matthew 18:8–9, and in a parallel form in Mark 9:43–48.

Part III. Awakening

Chapter 10. The Rhetoric of Revival

1. Edwards, *A Faithful Narrative of the Surprising Work of God . . . in Northampton and the Neighboring Towns . . .* (London, 1737), reprinted in *The Great Awakening* (New Haven: Yale University Press, 1972).

2. Edwards, *Selections,* 106. Perry Miller has a thorough discussion of Edwards' use of John Locke, and of the significance of this sermon, in *Jonathan Edwards,* 43–68.

3. Quoted in Miller, *Jonathan Edwards,* 51.

4. Quoted in Miller, *Jonathan Edwards*, 34, emphasis added.

5. Edwards, *Selections*, 161–162, 164–165. This sermon was first preached in Enfield, Connecticut in 1741.

6. Joseph Tracy, *The Great Awakening* (Boston, 1841), 216; quoted in Edwards, *Selections*, xvii.

7. Charles Chauncy, *Seasonable Thoughts on the State of Religion in New England* (Boston, 1743), 302, 324. Quoted in Edwards, *Selections*, xx, xxi. Conflict between rationalists and revivalists would continue, gaining fresh intensity during the "Second Great Awakening" in the early nineteenth century. At that time New England rationalists broke away from Congregationalism to form the Unitarian Church.

8. Edwards, *The Distinguishing Marks of a Work of the Spirit of God*, in *Great Awakening*, 248.

9. I use "displacement" in the psychoanalytic sense, "The shifting of an emotional affect . . . from an appropriate to an inappropriate object" (*The American Heritage Dictionary*).

10. Edwards, *A Faithful Narrative*, in *Great Awakening*, 151, 174–175, 183.

11. Edwards, *A Faithful Narrative*, in *Great Awakening*, 206–207.

Chapter 11. Jonathan's Experience

1. Edwards, "Personal Narrative," in *Selections*, 57.

2. Ola Elizabeth Winslow, *Jonathan Edwards 1703–1758* (New York: Collier Books, 1961), 48.

3. See "Of Insects" in Edwards, *Selections*, 3–10.

4. Miller, *Edwards*, 37.

5. Edwards, "Resolutions," in *Selections*, 38, 39, final emphasis added.

6. Edwards, *Selections*, 41, 42.

7. Edwards, "Personal Narrative," in *Selections*, 59.

8. Edwards, *Selections*, 60. He also recalls telling his father about these experiences, and receiving his father's approval.

9. Edwards, *Selections*, 61.

10. Edwards, *Selections*, 61.

11. Edwards, *Selections*, 63.

12. Edwards, "Personal Narrative," in *Selections*, 69.

13. For a somewhat different psychological interpretation of these same materials, see Richard L. Bushman, "Jonathan Edwards as Great Man: Identity, Conversion, and Leadership in the Great Awakening," *Encounter with Erikson: Historical Interpretation and Religious Biography*, ed. Donald Capps, Walter H. Capps, and M. Gerald Bradford (Santa Barbara, CA: Scholars Press, 1977), 217–252.

14. See Ephesians 5:21–33.

15. Amanda Porterfield, *Feminine Spirituality in America: from Sarah Edwards to Martha Graham* (Philadelphia: Temple University Press, 1980), 49. I am indebted to this fine study for several thoughts on Puritan sexuality.

16. Edwards, "Of Being," in *Selections*, 20.

17. Winslow, *Jonathan Edwards*, 139–140.

Chapter 12. Sarah's Experience

1. Both *The Distinguishing Marks of a Work of the Spirit of God*

(1741) and *Some Thoughts Concerning the Present Revival of Religion* (1742) are found in Edwards, *Great Awakening*.

2. Her account was printed in S. E. Dwight, *The Life of President Edwards* (New York: G. & C. & H. Carvill, 1830), 171–186.

3. Edwards, *Religious Affections*, 242–243.

4. There is an insightful treatment of Sarah in Amanda Porter-field, *Feminine Spirituality in America*. The one "biography" of Sarah Edwards is a disaster: Elisabeth D. Dodds, *Marriage to a Difficult Man* (Philadelphia: Westminster Press, 1971). This weaves a sentimental portrait from the occasional, stereo-typed, flattering remarks about Sarah in the writings of the Edwardses' many visitors. At the one point where the author has real information from Sarah herself, she reveals no under-standing of Sarah's religious experience: "Here we don't like her at all. The serene mother becomes limply needful. The patient wife comes to the end of her patience. The attractive hostess becomes grotesque—jabbering, hallucinating, idiotical-ly fainting. We are embarrassed for her" (95).

5. Edwards, *Some Thoughts*, in *Great Awakening*, 334.

6. Porterfield, *Feminine Spirituality*, 40.

7. Edwards, *Great Awakening*, 68.

8. Dwight, *Life*, 172, 173, 174. Her new confidence was accom-panied, however, by some morbid fantasies "of being chased from the town . . . and . . . left to perish with the cold," which would nevertheless not "in the least disturb the inex-pressible happiness and peace of my soul" (174). This masochism intensified later in her account.

9. Dwight, *Life*, 175, 176.

10. Dwight, *Life*, 178.

11. Dwight, *Life*, 180.

12. Dwight, *Life*, 181.

13. Dwight, *Life*, 183.

14. Dwight, *Life*, 184.

15. Dwight, *Life*, 185.

Chapter 13. The Body

1. Edwards, *Some Thoughts*, in *Great Awakening*, 335, 341.

2. Edwards, *Some Thoughts,* in *Great Awakening*, 300.

3. Edwards, *Religious Affections*, 132.

4. Edwards, *Some Thoughts*, in *Great Awakening*, 336, 338.

5. These sentences paraphrase Taylor Stoehr's characterization

of Paul Goodman's psychology in *Nature Heals,* xxii, quoted earlier, 71–72.

6. I will deepen my discussion of the biblical view of human personality in Book 3. In the brief discussion above I have followed Edwards and most Christian philosophers in using "soul" and "mind" interchangeably. I recognize that the notion of "soul" in traditional Christian philosophy also has an additional characteristic—permanence or immortality.

7. Edwards, *Religious Affections,* 234.

8. Winslow, *Jonathan Edwards,* 236.

Part IV. Identity

1. Martin Luther quoted in Erik H. Erikson, *Young Man Luther* (New York: W. W. Norton & Co., Inc. 1958), 244.

2. Samuel Terrien, *The Elusive Presence: The Heart of Biblical Theology* (San Francisco: Harper & Row, 1978).

Chapter 14. God's Enjoyment

1. Edwards, Misc. 749, quoted in Delattre, *Beauty and Sensibility,* 50, n. 20.

2. Edwards, Misc. 332 and Misc. 107, quoted in Delattre, *Beauty and Sensibility,* 170.

3. Edwards, Sermon on Luke 2:14, quoted in Delattre, *Beauty and Sensibility,* 170.

4. Delattre observes, "This aesthetic qualification of being-itself at its very center is perhaps the distinctive mark of his philosophical theology." Also, "It is by virtue of God's beauty that effulgence has priority over self-sufficiency in Edwards' conception of God." (Delattre, *Beauty and Sensibility,* 105, 169).

5. Edwards, "A Dissertation Concerning the End for Which God Created the World," in S. E. Dwight, *The Works of President Edwards* (New York: S. Converse, 1829), vol. 3, 20.

6. Edwards, *Works,* ed. Dwight, vol. 3, 18.

7. Edwards, Misc. 247, quoted in Delattre, *Beauty and Sensibility,* 177.

8. I will discuss nature's participation in the Fall in Book 3. Here the point that our perceptions of nature are clouded by human sin is sufficient for the argument.

9. Edwards, Misc. 1151, quoted in Delattre, *Beauty and Sensibility,* 177.

10. I will develop this biblical theme in Book 3 of this study.

11. Jürgen Moltmann, *God in Creation: A New Theology of Creation and the Spirit of God* (San Francisco: Harper & Row, 1985), 197.

12. John Muir, *John of the Mountains: The Unpublished Journals*, ed. Linnie Marsh Wolfe (Madison, WI: The University of Wisconsin Press, 1979), 213.

13. Saint Francis of Assisi, quoted in Edward A. Armstrong, *Saint Francis, Nature Mystic: The Derivation and Significance of the Nature Stories in the Franciscan Legend* (Berkeley: University of California Press, 1973), 239.

14. John Muir, Journal, 1972, 3–6; John Muir papers, Holt-Atherton Center for Western Studies, University of the Pacific, copyright 1984 Muir-Hanna Trust. See *Baptized into Wilderness*, 53.

15. Muir, *John of the Mountains*, 79–80.

16. Edwards, *Nature of True Virtue*, 15.

17. Delattre, *Beauty and Sensibility*, 168.

18. Edwards, *Religious Affections*, 298.

19. I continue this discussion in chapter 18.

20. Edwards, "An Essay on the Trinity," *Selections*, 378.

21. Edwards, Misc. 1151, quoted in Delattre, *Beauty and Sensibility*, 177.

Chapter 15. Experience of the Lord

1. Jonathan Edwards, "Extracts from his Private Writings," from *Works of President Edwards* (Leeds: Edward Baines, 1806), vol. 1, 33–34.

2. Edwards, Misc. 530, quoted in Delattre, *Beauty and Sensibility,* 36

3. Edwards, *Religious Affections*, 206.

4. Edwards, "A Divine and Supernatural Light," *Selections*, 108.

5. Historians generally credit awakened American Puritans and Presbyterians, however, with contributing energy to the movements which led to the American Revolution. In England, Methodism is credited with helping discipline the work force which was often docile under oppression in the developing industrial cities.

6. I will return to part of this concern in Book 4, where I will apply both biblical and Jeffersonian principles to suggest ways to integrate respect for nature into American culture and politics.

7. Edwards, *Religious Affections*, 206.

8. Erikson, *Young Man Luther*, 14, 15. Erikson summarized his theory of identity development in most of his books, stating it most clearly in *Childhood and Society*. In *Identity: Youth and Crisis*, he develops more adequately the social dimension of identity formation. First in *Young Man Luther* and later in *Gandhi's Truth*, he showed the prophetic personality wrestling with a contradiction until an insight is fashioned which welded individual wholeness to a drive for social reformation.

9. Erik H. Erikson, *Identity: Youth and Crisis* (New York: W.W. Norton & Co., Inc., 1968), 22.

10. Erikson, *Young Man Luther*, 254.

11. Erikson, *Identity: Youth and Crisis*, 142–150.

12. Erikson, *Identity: Youth and Crisis*, 40.

Chapter 16. Moral Beauty

1. Samuel Terrien commented on psalms which depict God's hiding:

> It was that very hiding which disclosed to them not only the meaning of their existence but also the intrinsic quality of divinity. The God of the psalmists made them live in this world, and they lived without using him. It is when man tries to grasp him that God veils himself. The *Deus revelatus* is the *Deus absconditus*.
>
> (Terrien, *Elusive Presence*, 326)

2. See above, 31–33.

3. Edwards, *A Treatise on Grace*, quoted in Delattre, *Beauty and Sensibility*, 50, note 22.

4. "*Sensuous* can refer to any of the senses but more often applies to those involved in aesthetic enjoyment of art, music, nature, and the like" (*The American Heritage Dictionary*).

> Sensuous was first used by Milton as a term descriptive of one thing which deals with sensations or has the power of evoking sensations as opposed to another thing which deals with ideas, and is intellectual in character (as, '[Poetry is] more simple, *sensuous*, and passionate [than rhetoric]'—Milton). . . . *Sensual* . . . now usually implies the gratification of the senses or the indulgence of the appetites through the impulsion of gluttony, lust, or other base motive; *sensuous*, on the contrary, implies the gratification of the senses (less often the indulgence of the appetites) for the sake of the aesthetic pleasure or the delight in beauty of color, sound, form, or the like, that is induced.

By permission. From*Webster's New Dictionary of Synonyms.*
© 1984 by Merriam-Webster, Inc., publisher of the Merriam-
Webster ® Dictionaries.

Edwards was consciously making the distinction from the
intellectual, as Milton. By elevating the sensuous to the soul,
he was also implicitly making the distinction from the "base"
and "bodily." For comment on Edwards' persistent use of the
image "sweetness" to convey the availability of God to human
affectionate perception, see above, 19.

5. See above, 19.

6. Edwards, Misc. 1151, quoted in Delattre, *Beauty and Sensibility*,
   177.

7. Edwards, *Religious Affections*, 253–254, 260, 273.

8. I am indebted for my interpretation of Psalm 18, and for the rendering "humility" in vs. 35, to Terrien, *Elusive Presence*, 283–290.

9. See Genesis 32:22–32, and 18:22–33.

10. Edwards, quoted in Delattre, *Beauty and Sensibility*, 50, 51.

Chapter 17. Wholeness

1. "Boundary" here does not refer to the meeting point of a person with a significant other, such as the "contact boundary"
   in the theory of Gestalt therapy. In this context, "boundary"
   means the limits of meaningful interaction with society,
   beyond which lies an unknown, unrecognized, or perhaps
   hostile world.

2. Erikson, *Identity: Youth and Crisis*, 81.

3. Erikson, *Young Man Luther*, 118, quoting Numbers 6:25–26.

4. Earlier, Wilhelm Reich had developed similar ideas in *The
   Mass Psychology of Fascism*, first published in 1946 (New
   York: Farrar, Straus & Giroux, 1970). See above, 69–70.

5. Erikson, *Identity: Youth and Crisis*, 75–76.

6. See above, 87–92.

Chapter 18. A Relevant Lord

1. Of course, such a categorical affirmation concerning reality,
   and a categorical negative about God, are no more "relativist"
   than a categorical affirmation of God's existence. But in popular thinking, a relativist critique of faith in God carries this
   implication.

2. Edwards, *Religious Affections*, 298. Condensed from "God is
   God, and distinguished from all other beings, and exalted
   above 'em, chiefly by his divine beauty."

3. Edwards, *Religious Affections*, 208.

4. Edwards, *Religious Affections*, 242–243.

5. Edwards, *Religious Affections*, 298. Edwards used the term "sensible knowledge," in contrast with "speculative knowledge," on page 272.

Part V. Nature

1. Reproduced in William Blake, *Songs of Innocence and of Experience*, introduction and commentary by Sir Geoffrey Keynes (London: The Orion Press, 1967), plate 44.

Chapter 19. Nature in Human Identity

1. Donald R. Griffin, Professor at the Rockefeller University, has written an excellent survey of animal capacities and of scientific efforts to suppress research on such capacities, in *Animal Thinking* (Cambridge, MA: Harvard University Press, 1984).

2. Wes Jackson, "A Search for the Unifying Concept for Sustainable Agriculture," in *Meeting the Expectations of the Land*, ed. Wes Jackson, Wendell Berry, and Bruce Colman (San Francisco: North Point Press, 1984), 223.

3. Henry David Thoreau, quoted in Worster, *Nature's Economy*, 85.

4. Leopold, *A Sand County Almanac*, 290.

5. Gary Snyder, "Good, Wild, Sacred," in *Meeting the Expectations of the Land*, ed. Jackson, et al., 206.

6. See 1 John 4:20.

7. See John 3:16.

Chapter 20. Christ in Nature

1. Edwards, *Selections*, 57; see above, 95.

2. Edwards, *Selections*, 69; see above, 98–100.

3. Edwards, *Images or Shadows of Divine Things* (New Haven: Yale University Press, 1948), 137

4. Edwards, "Concerning the End for Which God Created the World," in *Works*, ed. Dwight, vol. 3, 23.

5. Edwards, Misc. 108, quoted in Delattre, *Beauty and Sensibility*, 181.

6. In the formal sacraments which Christians associate with Christ, natural ingredients help believers experience, sensuously, God's relationship to us. In baptism, the cleansing water gives experience of God's forgiveness washing away our sins;

in the Eucharist, bread and wine help us take in the promise of Christ's presence. We are encouraged to "Taste and see that the LORD is good!" (Psalm 34:8, RSV). Natural ingredients convey sacramental experience only when the believer's attention is directed to the Lord. A good swim does not usually convey God's forgiveness. A Eucharist which grows into a good meal may, by calling attention to itself, distract from Christ. This was apparently one of the problems among the Corinthians that Paul had to address (1 Corinthians 11:20–34). Churches, perhaps overanxious about sensual distraction, have tended to weaken the sacraments by substituting sprinkling for immersion, wafers for bread, or grape juice for wine.

7. Edwards, Misc. 108, quoted in Delattre, *Beauty and Sensibility*, 82.

8. See Book 1, *Baptized into Wilderness*, particularly chapters 2 and 10.

Chapter 21. Ecology Fulfilled

1. Moltmann, *God in Creation*, 139.

2. Charles Birch and John B. Cobb, Jr., *The Liberation of Life: From the Cell to the Community* (Cambridge: Cambridge University Press, 1981), 144. This book develops an argument for valuing life in proportion to consciousness and creativity, based on Charles Hartshorne's process philosophy.

3. Leopold, quoted in Susan L. Flader, *Thinking Like a Mountain: Aldo Leopold and the Evolution of an Ecological Attitude toward Deer, Wolves and Forests* (Lincoln, NE: University of Nebraska Press, 1978), 33.

4. Jackson, "A Search for the Unifying Concept," in *Meeting the Expectations of the Land*, ed. Jackson, et al., 224.

5. John Muir, *To Yosemite and Beyond: Writings from the Years 1863 to 1875*, ed. Robert Engberg and Donald Wesling (Madison, Wisconsin: University of Wisconsin Press, 1980), 121.

6. Human ethical responsibility for domesticated lands and livestock was clearly recognized in the Bible, as I will discuss in Book 3. I will consider ethics of domestication appropriate to modern culture in Book 4.

7. See, for example, Bill Devall and George Sessions, *Deep Ecology: Living as if Nature Mattered* (Salt Lake City: Gibbs M. Smith, Inc., 1985), where this perspective grows amid a great many valuable insights.

8. Moltmann, *God in Creation*, 51. Moltmann (328 n.) derived this

idea from Julian Huxley's definition of humanity as "evolution becomes conscious of itself," an idea also developed by Teilhard de Chardin. The important truth here is partially buried beneath the hierarchical notion of humanity as the goal, purpose, or fruition of creation. I try to avoid this hierarchical perspective in recognition of the diverse values in ecological life.

9. *Baptized into Wilderness*, 44.

10. Birch and Cobb, *The Liberation of Life*, 65.

11. René Dubos, *A God Within* (New York: Charles Scribner's Sons, 1972), 135.

12. See Ian L. McHarg, *Design with Nature* (Garden City, NY: Doubleday & Co., 1971), 72–73.

13. René Dubos, *So Human an Animal* (New York: Charles Scribner's Sons, 1968), 200.

14. Dr. James E. Hansen, Goddard Space Flight Center, National Aeronautics and Space Administration, testifying before the Senate Environmental Pollution Subcommittee, as quoted in *The New York Times*, Sunday, 15 June, 1986, E–6.

15. I develop this discussion in Book 3, Chapter 21.

Chapter 22. Death in the Okavango

1. K. L. Tinley, *An Ecological Reconnaissance of the Moremi Wildlife Reserve, Botswana* (Okovango [sic] Wildlife Society, 1973), 108.

2. Alfred Lord Tennyson, stanza LVI of "In Memoriam," *Poems of Tennyson*, ed. Jerome Hamilton Buckley (Boston: Houghton Mifflin Co., 1958).

3. See Botswana Society, *Proceedings of the Symposium on the Okavango Delta and its Future Utilization*, August 30th to September 2nd, 1976 (Gaborone, Botswana: Botswana Society).

Index

BIBLICAL CITATIONS